Crossing a Different Bridge
An Oklahoma Memoir

Judith Tate O'Brien

Cover photograph:
Old Highway 66 Bridge Over North Canadian River, Oklahoma County
© 2009 by Josh McCullock

Cover Design by JLC Mish, 2009
Book Design: Mongrel Empire Press using iWork Pages.

MONGREL EMPIRE PRESS
NORMAN, OKLAHOMA, UNITED STATES OF AMERICA

WWW.MONGRELEMPIREPRESS.COM

This publisher is a proud member of

[clmp]

COUNCIL OF LITERARY MAGAZINES & PRESSES
w w w . c l m p . o r g

Founding Member
**OKLAHOMA
SMALL PRESS
ASSOCIATION**

Table of Contents

Acknowledgements

Some poems in this memoir have been previously published:

"It was the age of boom, bubble, and burst" was first published as "Oklahoma Boom Towns" in *Oklahoma Today*, Jan/Feb 2009: 7.

"My mother's sweet peas twined the fence" was first published as "Fence" in *Atlanta Review*, Summer 2008:11.

They hung on nails near battered buckets" was first published as "Milk Habits" in *Connecticut River Review* 21.1: 54.

"I wasn't a bride was first published as "Coming to the End of a Path" in *Connecticut River Review* 1996: 64."

"A green sky . . ." was first published as "Nuns Remembered" in Byline, March 2005: 57.

"Even after I knew" was first published as "At the Krebs-McAlester Mines"in *Oklahoma Today, Jan/Feb 2007: 72.*

"Maybe it was the lilt of *el* or the lingering *ar*" was first published as "Cellar Door" in *Nimrod*, 51.2: 33.

"Today my hands are liver-spotted and rope veined. So much" was first published as "Something Inside Me Wants To Kneel Down" in *Poem* #99: 15.

"Indeed all that remains of the monastery" was first published as "Cemetery at Sacred Heart, Oklahoma" in *By the Grace of Ghosts,* co-authored with Jane Taylor, published by Village Books Press, 2003.

"Neither of us suspected malignant" as "Sisters"; "The boarding school laundry room" as "Uniform Shirts"; and "He began reciting" as "Catechism Lesson," were first published in the chapbook *Mythic Places*, ByLine Press, 2000.

Special Thanks

My husband, Gene, set this project in motion, gave me space and time to work and buoyed me when I doubted the project's worthwhileness.

Jane Taylor, my writing partner, lent both practical suggestions and poetic sensibilities while I worked on this memoir.

Maxine Fightmaster proofread the manuscript with a grammarian's eagle eye and a historian's acumen. Maxine's study of Oklahoma history, particularly of the Potawatomi tribe, was very helpful.

Readers Don and Linda Baustert and Jane and David Best provided valuable feedback.

Marcia Preston, award-winning novelist and former editor, read the manuscript with an eye to prose flow.

Todd Best helped design the cover.

Nota Bene: Except for immediate family members, names have been changed.

For Colette, Joan, Ann, Kathleen, Lori

Crossing A Different Bridge

I picture the young lovers trundling south from Michigan, she in a stylish cloche and a voile dress with butterfly sleeves; he dapper with a tiny red feather tucked in the band of his fedora. They rode in his enclosed Model T Ford. Acre by acre, the land browned. At first my mother didn't notice the landscape shift from lush to sparse. The realization of change was unexpected, as change often is. Where were the trees? I like to think she was poet enough to see the beauty in a sycamore standing solitary in a field, to notice how scrub oaks lift chunks of sky along with leaves in their twisted arms.

In the 1920's, automobiles shared highways with horses and horse-drawn wagons. When my father passed wagons loaded with people or hay, I imagine he honked—*ooga, ooga*—and waved in a cloud of dust. He felt proud to be driving his own car. Despite Henry Ford's dream, not every family owned one. My father would have wanted travelers to notice both his car and his young bride. "When we get to Chicago," he told her, "we'll pick up Highway 66. Paved all the way to Tulsa."

The trip took four days and three nights. For the lovers, evenings didn't come soon enough.

They spent each night in one of the tourist cabins which had sprung up to accommodate car travel. "The motel," people would later say, "was invented by Henry Ford."

From Tulsa, my father cut across Oklahoma on the "mother road." Crossing the Canadian River on one of Highway 66's iron bridges must have felt to the girl who would become my mother like crossing an ocean to the Land No Return. When Ed wheeled into the oil camp in Estelline, Texas, my mother beheld her future home. No flowers or grass. Goat-head stickers along the fence. A tinfoil sun baking the hardpan. The thick hot stench of oil and its byproducts. Shotgun houses, each with a dirt path leading to a lopsided privy.

The only color was provided by the gas flare which rose on a long stem of pipe and jittered red-orange like a poppy in a breeze.

It was no place for new lovers.

Such a long way from her dad's asparagus farm in Paw Paw, Michigan. Years later, I would travel to Michigan and sleep in the room she'd slept in. It was a small room and square. A blue-and-white ceramic basin and pitcher sat on the wash stand. Damask curtains billowed in a gentle breeze at the window she had looked through.

What a contrast!

But my mother almost had to like oil field camps. There was no returning to Michigan. Her dad had strongly objected to his only child's marital choice. He had pointed out the age difference: Ed almost 40; Lois 18. He had pointed out the differences in religion: Ed completely unchurched—"a nothing"; Lois a Catholic. Educational difference: Lois a graduate from a high-school taught by strict French nuns; Ed a 4th grade education—and that in an Indian boarding school. Ed was a two-bit gambler who only occasionally worked the harvest. Look at his hands.

Since reason did not dissuade her, my grandfather resorted to anger. He ordered his daughter to stop seeing the man she loved. Impossible. He warned Ed not to step foot on the property.

The lovers were stubborn.

Defeated, my grandfather said, "Think of your dead mother. She would have wanted you to stay here." Then, a final shot, a warning really: "Remember, Lois, if you leave, you can't come back home. 'If you make the bed, you have to lie in it." He would not have known those were the last words he'd say to her.

By eloping, my mother escaped her red-haired father's temper and broke his heart.

It was in Estelline that my gambling dad traded in his card-playing hands for calluses. The couple sold the car and bought a bed. She sewed curtains. Dust blew. I was conceived on gritty sheets and born in April. It was 1928.

From Estelline, my mother, father, and I moved to various oil-boom towns in Oklahoma.

It was the Age of Boom, Bubble, & Bust. Oil workers
trucked loads of drill pipe down red-dirt roads.
                    Derricks plunged iron tongues
underground and reared tall as dinosaurs against
Oklahoma's blazing sky. Boom towns tumbled
                like tumbleweeds
at oil rigs' feet. One-lane roads linked slush pits
to saloons and to one-room hotels with unlikely names
              like Hawaiian Breeze.
Shamrock and its tumbleweed townlets—Alright,
Downright, Damright (no kidding!), and Justright—
              learned how soon boom
can bubble and bust. On maps today, Shamrock remains
a rusty dot on state maps. But its townlets have been reduced
              to fistfuls of red dust.

We never lived in Damright. My dad would have loved that. Among oil field workers, cussing was a prerequisite that ranked right up there with guts and brawn. My father was a talented cusser. How else could he have handled the winch line that chewed off his finger, or responded to the day fire climbed up the derrick faster than Dean could clamber down, or got through the day Big Dale stumbled into the slush pit? Yes, he would have loved to be able to say "Your damn right we live in Damright."

As it was, however, we lived in Seminole, Wewoka, Bethany, Oklahoma City, Shawnee, Maud. My mother's dad had warned her, "He'll haul you around the country. You'll live like gypsies."

The camp I remember most clearly was situated on the outskirts of Maud, Oklahoma. We called the place Blue Heaven because the houses and privies were painted blue.

In the beginning of commercial oil drilling, single men—notoriously a rowdy bunch—made up the oilfield workforce, leaving a large number of capable, married workers untapped. So some oil-company owners built company houses where married workers could bring their families. The camp at Maud was one such place. Company houses were usually painted a color that identified the owner. Thus, camps with blue houses would belong to, say, Mr. Barnes and yellow-painted houses would belong to, say, Mr. Coyle. Perhaps the color-coding system was only a brief page in State history. I've seen only one reference to it.

In Blue Heaven, I grew up hearing oil-field jargon: pump house, drilling mud, bottom-well pump, pump station, pump jack, crow's nest, gusher. At an early age, I knew by heart the story of Ruby Darby, the exotic dancer who, wearing a fur coat with (reportedly) nothing under it, drove her red convertible from boom town to boom town where she entertained oil field workers. Ruby Darby was memorialized in oil-field lingo: a darby meant a gusher. "It's hard to stop a darby," drillers would say, " but, by God, what a strike."

Since the women who lived in Blue Heaven had no jobs outside the camp and only infrequent reasons to go beyond the confines, and since their husbands often rushed through supper and then spent hours drinking beer and playing poker in the tin warehouse, their wives did what women down through the centuries have done: they created a life among themselves. In that world, no one locked her door. No one knocked. Coffee always perked in the percolator. Their world had its own language (it was okay to say damn but not goddamn, kids addressed neighbors as aunt and uncle); its own dress code (nothing fancy, aprons required, bare feet acceptable); its own approved conversation topics (recipes, complaints about husbands, Bob Wills and his Texas Playboys). And, of course, the camp women gossiped—that age-old form of story-telling. In a way, Aunt Faye cheated; she staved off juicy tittle-tattle by providing the senate of women graphic details about the origin of her bruised arm or her black eye.

My father was deeply in love with my mother. She sometimes sat on his lap after supper while their children hung around like voyeurs watching him stub out his cigarette and run his hands down her cheeks and around her breasts. He often hastened kitchen cleanup by drying dishes and tossing the dishwater out the back door.

The nights my father played cards and drank beer with the other men, he came home by 11. He'd tumble into bed claiming to be dead tired. But clearly he wasn't too tired to talk with my mother. I remember being lulled to sleep by the low murmur of their voices.

Once I heard my mother say to a neighbor, "I'd rather be an old man's darling than a young man's slave." I cringed. Even at age five, I knew it was impolitic to say such a thing to a young woman who was almost certainly married to a young man. Mistake or not, my mother seemed to thrive on my father's delight in her. Looking back, I think their mutual enchantment made it possible for my mother to live almost content in the camp.

By 1935 my sister, Lois, was old enough to share the big bed with me. She was a beautiful child. I often heard people comment on her soft black curls, large dark eyes, long lashes. I was very proud of her. She was named for my mother, Lois—also beautiful.

My father was proud of mama. She wore makeup. She always wore hose and pumps. She had only finished high-school, but my father thought attending a school run by nuns from Canada was equivalent to attending Oxford. She played the violin and taught my sister and me to read music. She could speak French. He thought she was both beautiful and brilliant.

But the very things that made my father proud of his wife made her something of a misfit in the camp.

> In summer in the hour or so between doing supper dishes
> and catching fireflies, us oil-patch kids liked to lie
> under a porch in the cool dirt, poke roly-poly bugs
> as some kid's mama walked from her smoky kitchen
> to a porch-chair just over our heads. She'd carry a jar of tea
> for herself and a talkative neighbor. Sprawled on our
> bellies on ground that hadn't been sun-scorched, we
> nearly dozed to the middle-C monotony of their voices.
> Occasionally, as if by prearrangement, all six mamas
> would meet on one porch, say Aunt Beulah Mae's.
> At such times, I liked to scramble from underneath,
> stand eye-level to the porch, and connect our mamas'
> voices to our mamas' feet. *I hear Old Man Barnes is gonna*
> *drill a new well over by Seminole*: (that would belong
> to a pair of bare feet); *I'll be damned if I'll move back*
> *there* vowed carpet slippers; and so it went—two sets
> of bare feet, one pair of leatherette slippers, a pair of men's
> shoes and my mother's nearly wordless black pumps.

The camp women may have felt superior to my mother. But they were kind. She was young. She was ignorant about the things that mattered in camp living. She couldn't cook so Aunt Bessie showed her how to fry pork chops and "whip up a mess of biscuits" which of course demanded gravy. She needed a lesson in gravy.

I remember the day Aunt Rachel, my father's oldest sister, visiting us from Oklahoma City, taught my mother the proper way to mop. "You use way too much water," I heard her say. "Leaving puddles is a sign of poor housekeeping." She also scolded mama for letting the icebox drip-pan overflow.

The drip-pan was kept under the ice-box to catch the melt from the block of ice which cooled food. Mama often forgot to empty it. But she became a skilled mopper. Maybe that's why she did it so often. Actually, I preferred my mother's watery method. I loved to watch her black pumps reflected in the wet linoleum. Now I wonder if mopping had been a kind of escape for her. The rhythm could be mesmerizing: *swish-wring-dry, swish-wring-dry.*

My mother found ways to add color to camp life. She and our next-door neighbor, Aunt Mae, planted flowers along the back fence between our two houses.

> My mother's sweet peas twined the fence behind
> our house like lines of lyric poetry. Each pink-
>
> flushed morning, still in chenille robe, she kissed
> my father, handed him his lunch, then sat and drank
> two dreamy cups of coffee. She kneaded egg
> shells and coffee grounds into the stubborn soil
>
> and, humming something sexy, shaped the earth
> into soft fertile curves. Even there in that
> sepia-toned compound, the pampered plants climbed
> up and beyond the fence that tried and failed to curb
>
> my mother's need for color. Buds swelled and opened pink
> mouths. They spoke to her in a language sweet and secret.

I remember Mother cutting bouquets of sweet-peas and placing them in Mason jars. We'd eat fried potatoes at a supper table made elegant and faintly fragrant with flowers. Lois and I thought the bouquets were nice, but since I hadn't grown up in my mother's home surrounded by bird baths and day lilies, I didn't yet know people need beauty.

My father came home from work smelling like sweat and oil, a thick man-odor. He parked his rig in front of the blue house where Mother was inside cooking supper. When Lois and I saw his truck, we ran to him and demanded to be lifted and "whiskered"—an affectionate face-rubbing that left us giggling and somewhat raw-cheeked.

One year, my mother began spending most of every day with Mrs. Graham* who lived across the highway. Mrs. Graham had cancer. (We called her Mrs. instead of Aunt because she did not live in Blue Heaven.) Lois and I went with Mother. She sent us to play outside, but I—nicknamed "Big Ears" by my father—usually slipped back inside

"Here, Irene," I'd hear my mother coax after fixing some broth or tea, "try just a little sip. You need to keep your strength up."

Some camp women disapproved of my mother striking up a friendship with someone outside the camp. I of the Big Ears once heard Aunt Betty Lou sniff, "I guess we're not good enough for her."

My father worried about his wife's health. She came home from Mrs. Graham's house tired. When my father fussed about her spending so much time and energy with a woman he didn't know, my mother fussed right back.

My father would begin gently. "Hon, I'm worried about you. You ought to see the circles under your eyes. You're all fagged out."

She'd stand her ground, so he'd push to the next level. "Lois, you shouldn't drag the kids across the road like that. You never know when a heavy truck is coming."

When that didn't work, he'd raise his voice. "By God, Lois, you're killing yourself. I won't have you going over to that old woman's house! I won't have it! You're not to go again!"

He should have remembered how she reacted when her dad forbade her to see my father. She left that time. She'd leave again.

_____

We must have traveled by train because my mother and I ended up in St. Louis with someone my mother called Aunt Johnnie. This memory is very foggy. I don't know how old I was. Three? Where was Lois? She must have remained in the camp, probably with Aunt Mae.

Aunt Johnnie lived on the third floor of a big apartment building close to train tracks. Several times a day, the building shook as the train rumbled past. My bed folded up into the wall. I found that nifty. Otherwise I didn't like being there at all. I couldn't go outside without my mother's going with me. And even then, I had to play on concrete sidewalks.

Being separated from my father was like living in a house without a roof. So unsafe. I felt shaky inside.

Left alone, I began to touch myself—without, I must say, any comfort. Years later, as a therapist, I asked a man how he had coped with his mother's suicide. His blunt answer: "I masturbated." I wonder if children try to connect with a missing parent by exploring the source of their own being. The doorway through which they'd come.

Maybe a week at Aunt Johnnie's passed before I woke up to find my father magically at the breakfast table.

I could tell by Aunt Johnnie's mouth that she liked neither my father nor my mother's plan to return home with him.

On the way home, we spent two nights at tourist cabins. The unease between my parents settled in my gut. When I threw up they both bent over me, discussing remedies for their sick child. United. Everything was suddenly okay then. Relief unlocked the tension in my gut and I was well. Oh, the power of a child! And the awful responsibility.

Since backseat riding exacerbated my proneness to car sickness, I was allowed to sit between my parents in the front seat of the borrowed car. I slept while their voices wove a friendly roof over my head.

During that trip home, I learned how responsive the body is to emotional climate. After feeling cold during my parents' brief separation, I felt warm.

When I was about five, we moved to a house just across the road from Blue Heaven. My father bought a second-hand upright piano for my pregnant mother. On the day I'm remembering I stood at the front screen door and witnessed the "breaking" of a horse. Lois was outside. My mother was playing a Brahms piece on the piano. Maybe it was the incongruity—music behind me and harshness before me—that gives this memory such clarity. Two men had tied the horse to a tree and blindfolded it with a red rag—the kind my father tied to drill pipes when his load extended beyond the truck bed. The men beat the horse with big branches until the animal bucked and whinnied. The men shouted and cussed and beat some more. Finally the horse's front legs folded. "Stop it! Stop," I sobbed so loud, my mother came over. She gently pulled me back and closed the wooden door. "Oh," was all she said. My tears had turned the awful scene into a water color, the horse's head-covering into a blur of red. "The horse fell down," I told my mother. "It fell down and turned into a red kite."

"Maybe it will fly away," she said.

On that day, I became aware of two things. One: I could change the way I looked at things. Two: grownups can't stop awful things from happening. My mother hadn't liked what the men were doing, but she'd seemed to take their act for granted. A shrug.

Almost every day, my sister, Lois, and I went across the seldom-traveled dirt road to Blue Heaven to play with Edith, Bill, Max, and the rest of the camp kids. In our minds, we still lived in Blue Heaven. The day my brother, Ed, was born, Aunt Mae came to our house to help my mother. In fact, Aunt Mae or another camp woman came almost every day for several weeks after the delivery. Sometimes my mother stayed in bed all day. Daddy was caught between excitement about his newborn and concern for his wife. I of the Big Ears heard Aunt Mae whisper the word cancer. I didn't understand the word, but by her tone, I understood its dark heaviness.

The baby, Ed, (Bud to us) was blonde. "How did we get a Swede from an Indian man and a French girl," my father would ask, lifting Bud as if he were showing off the Hope Diamond.

My mother slowly regained enough strength to go about her usual duties. My father helped. On Sundays he cooked. He was a better cook than Mother was. She specialized in fried pork chops and potatoes which usually left the kitchen smoky and lard-smelling. My father mashed potatoes with lots of butter, salt, and pepper. One Sunday he cooked poke greens. "My mom used to fix poke," he told us. He made biscuits. We had squirrel and, once, fish. As I remember this, I wonder if he found my mother's cooking inadequate. I never heard him complain.

During that period, Mother rested a lot. Nearly every morning during that time, I woke up feeling cold. But if Mother came smiling into the kitchen, I ran outside to play. Who needed a sweater?

When my brother was three, he began sleeping with Lois and me. As the oldest and self-appointed ruler, I drew imaginary lines down the country of tumbled mattress and instructed the other two inhabitants not to trespass into my section. Of course they committed acts of civil disobedience in the dark. We quarreled. Our father would call, "Quiet down in there, Babies" Sometimes he'd call in mock sternness say, "Order in the court." We giggled every time. (He called Lois and me "Baby" even after we were grown.)

Sometimes, though, he'd come into our room and say softly, "You need to be quiet in here, Babies. Your mother is sick."

In the 1930s, abdominal cancer was treated with radium. Our mother's cancer was never cured; but off and on for several years, it seemed to go into a kind of remission. At those times, she went about life as usual. Then the house sang.

It must have been during an extended period of remission that I overheard my mother say to Daddy, "Eddie Mae will be in the third grade next year and I don't want her to be a kid who changes schools every year. If you're going to take Barnes up on that job in Oklahoma City, this is the time to do it."

Basically, the new job was not so much my father's as it was his family's. The added job meant we would move into a four-room house located on Sunnylane in the Oklahoma City equipment yard where the presence of a family was meant to discourage would-be thieves. It also meant extra income. All we had to do was live there! That and be vigilant.

We entered a brief happy period. In many ways, it seems like someone else's story. My mother seemed healthy. We had a car. A tan Chevrolet. We even had a rug in the front room. To keep the dust down, my mother swept the rug with a wet broom. About once a month, she dressed up in her gold-colored dress with fake-fur trim at the sleeves and neck, and she and my father went dancing at the VFW hall. While my father was at work in the Seminole Yard, my mother used the car to run errands. For Lois, Bud, and me, riding in our very own car was living in the lap of luxury. Every time Mother drove the three miles to the grocery store, we'd beg to ride along. "Go 40, Mama," we'd plead. And she would. She was a daredevil.

I remember watching my mother polish her nails. One day, she let me sit on her lap while she polished mine.   Afterward she spread my hand out beside hers and showed me the similarities in shape. My mental picture of the event is as grainy as an old photograph, but the smells of nail polish and of my mother's body are still sharp. Even now, the smell of nail polish brings the memory of that afternoon rushing back like a movie.

Today my hands are liver-spotted and rope veined. So much
history in so small a space. Both index fingers lean inward.
Like my mother's. She had her mother's hands. Three generations
of bent fingers and long lifelines. As a child, I imagined
lifelines as narrow rails stretching between the city of Here,
located at the base of the thumb, and the town of There where
the map disappeared over the edge of the palm. My mother
has traveled to the unfathomable town of There. I still live in the city
of Here. My hands have combed my sister's curls and stretched
octaves at a piano. They've milked cows in a monastery's old barn.
They've held the books that held the words stored now in my wrinkled
brain. Today I study my palm to see if there's movement
yet on the rail. There is. This is when someone inside me wants
to kneel down. The train is coming, windows lit.

One warm December day, the postman brought a package to our house. My mother's cheeks grew pink. Little rosy circles that I knew meant pleasure.

"Who's it from? Who? Who?" I danced around the kitchen table with excitement. A package? To our house?

"It's from my father."

My mother had a Daddy? Where had he been all my life. She told me he lived in Michigan in a town called Paw Paw. His name was Jack Kitchen

Over and over, I chanted: "Jack Kitchen. Paw Paw, Michigan." I loved rhyme.

Forty years later, trying to make contact with a grandfather I'd never met, I would remember the rhyme and my repetition of it. That's the address I wrote on the envelope. "Jack Kitchen. Paw Paw, Michigan."

My mother let me unwrap the package while she finished reading the letter stuffed inside the box from the mysterious man from a mysterious place. He had sent us a plaster-of-paris doorstop shaped like a kitten with glass eyes and a glittery collar.

How had Jack Kitchen known where we lived? Maybe my mother had written him. Or maybe my father. I don't know. But on the day my mother received that package from her father, I witnessed the transformative power of reconciliation. My pink-cheeked mother mopped the floor humming and, although I didn't know then about the rupture that had happened between them, I could tell she was happy.

A few days later the wind slammed shut the kitchen door and broke the doorstop to smithereens.

My mother enrolled my sister and me in music classes: violin for Lois, accordion for me. To balance the heavy accordion, I had to rear so far back, my mother said I looked like a flamenco dancer. My mother could play both instruments. Since we had a car, she drove Lois and me to lessons at a studio in downtown Oklahoma City. But our musical education was cut short when Mother became sick again.

It was as if clouds blocked the sun. In fact, the house itself felt cloudy. I remember wearing a sweater even in early September.

Three or four different times that year, my mother went to the hospital for radium treatments. My father hired a woman, Lizzie, to take care of us when Mother was in the hospital and to help her when she came home.

After the first treatment and a few days' rest at home, my mother was able to get out of bed. She enrolled me in Crooked Oak School. I must have been in the third grade. She wanted to meet my teacher. After her visit, my teacher said to me, "Your mother looks awful." I thought my mother was beautiful. The teacher's comment left me feeling ashamed.

The feeling of shame grew more intense the day my mother came home from the beauty shop with a boyish hair cut. I was hopscotching with kids from across the street. "How do you like my new hair style," she asked. In my little-girl heart, I knew she hated what the radium had done to her once-luxuriant hair. I knew she wanted to be beautiful to me. I looked away from her. "It's nice."

I knew the cruel lie broke her heart.

Not long after that, I overheard Lizzie complaining to a neighbor about having to change the dressing on my mother's incision—an "open, bloody mess that smells like a dead horse."

My siblings and I stayed outside as much as possible, partly because we didn't want to be in the house with Lizzie and partly because when Mother was home we were constantly shushed.

Worst of all was when Mother could get up and became a stranger. I didn't understand that disease and how its treatment can affect personality.

I remember one day in particular: Mother was out of bed that day. I'd broken some Christmas ornaments and she came outside red-faced, grabbed me hard by my arm and slapped my bare legs. I cried more from shock than being spanked. Who was that woman?

During that time, Lois, Bud, and I spent nearly all day outdoors. I remember straddling a pump jack and pretending it was a winged horse that would carry me to a planet where cancer was unknown.

Finally, my mother didn't get out of bed. My father had to go to work, but he drove home every night.

> Every night for months he rushed
> from the oil rig in stained work shirt
> and bailed into his truck's metal jail,
> a prisoner rushing, rushing, reckless
> in his rush, to my mother sentenced
> to life in a sheet-and-blanket cell,
> a prisoner who imprisoned ruby
> clots in her blazing belly, and roads
> purred beneath the truck's big tires
> and the trucker, my father, strangled
> the steering wheel with thick hands
> and stomped on the gas pedal until
> the highway flowed like a flaming
> brazier cutting a covenant between
> her life and her death, and nothing
> was real except night, the rhinestone
> stars, and the lump lodged in his
> chest like smoldering coal, emerald
> embers rising into the amethyst
> sky and the dazzling galaxy, and he
> would rush into the house and lay
> the night god's gems beside her, as
> if, kneeling there, shoulders shaking,
> he could swap them for the bleeding
> jewels shining inside her bloated belly.

One day my father took the three of us into Mother's bedroom. It was a Thursday and he'd come home earlier than usual. Mother asked, "How was Sunday school today?" None of us answered. Not only did we never attend church, but it wasn't even Sunday. The visit felt creepy. The only Mother-like moment was when she reached out to touch us and call our names. She tried to stroke our heads, but after mine, her hand fell limp.

My father began coming home in the early afternoons. He sometimes carried Mother to the car and settled her, oh so carefully with pillows and quilts. He drove out into the country so she could get fresh air and hear birdsong because she thought it came closest to the violin music she loved. All his attention was for Mother. If total attention was a kind of prayer, my father prayed. Clearly, she was his music.

On the days my father came home early, he picked me up from school. Otherwise I walked. At a certain place en route, I could see our house.

One night I dreamed I was walking home from school, but when I reached the top of the familiar spot, our house wasn't there! The Equipment Yard was there, the pipes and pumps and warehouse. But the spot where our home was supposed to sit was empty! A white square. My heart pounded. In my dream, a carbon-copy hill lay before me and I ran up it. Again, no home. Erased! I don't know how many times I ran up that hill and found no home before I awoke exhausted and trembling. In the dark, the dream became a stone. A dull black stone that settled in my throat. How could a dream be so heavy? I felt suffocated.

Two days after the dream, Daddy stayed home from work. That afternoon, he came outside and called me. "Eddie Mae." I was walking the length of a long pipe, waving my arms for balance. I pretended not to hear. He called again and I slowly went to him

"Your mother is going to die," he said. His chin trembled then, and he put big oil-stained hands over his face. The sounds he made were like car wrecks. I was both fascinated and terribly frightened. My strong father crying! Finally, he stopped making the terrible sounds and said, "Maybe we shouldn't tell the other two yet." We! I knew he'd made me almost an adult. The stone left in my throat from the dream sank to the muddy bottom of my belly. I actually found it difficult to stand erect.

I rejoined my sister and brother and said, "Mama's going to die." Maybe telling was my way of trying to reject my new role.

That night, my father's brother, our Uncle Travis, woke us. He was drunk, sitting on the edge of our bed, sobbing.

The funeral was a blur. I remember someone lifting me up, asking if I'd like to kiss my mother. I shook my head. The stone woman in the gold-colored dress with fake fur trim was not my mother. The smell of lilies thickened the air and made me nauseated. I tried to stay away from Aunt Rachel because I gagged when the smell of Lady Ester face powder mixed with the scent of lilies. Mournful music wafted eerily from behind a purple curtain.

Back at the house after the funeral, I lay on a divan and wouldn't eat despite Aunt Rachel's coaxing. Aunt Rachel seemed suddenly to have walked on stage to take care of the situation. My father was nowhere in sight. Once, I saw his back and tried to get to him through the fog of neighbors. The man talking to him was saying, "We'd love to take that one." He jerked a thumb toward the doorway. My beautiful little sister stood there. I'd never been jealous before. I stood very still. What would my father say?

"No way. I'll not separate them. The last thing Lois said to me was, 'Ed, keep them all together.' She told me to put them in a Catholic boarding school."

"Even the boy? How old is the little tyke?"

"Just turned five."

We sat in the boarding school parlor. I was 8, Lois, 6, Bud, 5. The linoleum floor had been waxed and buffed to mirror-like gloss. My chair, oceanic and high-armed, seemed to swallow me.

I gazed into the mirrored floor. The world there was upside down. So was the world above. We were characters in an Alice-in-Wonderland story. Any minute we would all sink into the floor and be upright again. But that didn't happen. An upside-down nun listened while Daddy talked. I watched him in the floor. He kept fingering the brim of his hat, turning it around and around. My father uneasy? Was he afraid of her, too? I'd never been around nuns and wondered if an entire woman lived inside the mysterious and voluminous garb.

The nuns who staffed St. Joseph's Boarding School and Academy belonged to the Franciscan Order whose Motherhouse was in Glen Riddle,

Pennsylvania. The school had grown from day students only to day students plus boarders, and from four nuns and a frame building in 1892 to 12 nuns in the red brick building we knew in 1936.

My upside down father and the nun in the shiny parlor must have discussed the work we would do to help defray the cost of tuition. Bud would sweep the basement porch; Lois would clean the music rooms; I would help in the kitchen.

I hadn't comprehended that my father was going away without us until the big door closed leaving him on the outside and the three of us alone with the nun. In my chest a space emptied.

Calling us poor motherless children, the nun, Sister Simeon, led Lois and me to a long room she called a dormitory. Rows of beds! All with white spreads.

"Try to get some sleep now. Get into your nighties. I'll have someone bring you a cup of hot tea."

The bed felt enormously lonely. At home, the three of us slept together in a double bed. I wondered how my little brother was faring. Was he in a dormitory, too? Was someone going to bring him hot tea?

The tea was good. I had never before tasted hot tea.

Exhaustion put me into a dreamless sleep. Someone gentle shook me awake. "You hungry? It's time for supper." A girl about my age, Jane Raynor (her real name), led Lois and me to the dining room. "It's called a refectory," Jane told us.

Refectory etiquette bewildered me. The boarders stood, eight at a table, to say grace, after which there was a synchronized flutter of hands. Forehead, chest, shoulders. Then a clatter of chairs but no talking until Sister Evelyn jingled a bell. Whoever sat at the head of the table filled the plates which were passed down until each child was served. Across the room at the boys' table, I finally spotted my little brother, his feet dangling, the smallest boy there. I hadn't seen him since the door had closed between us and Daddy. Bud, who was a finicky eater and probably, like Lois and me, also constipated with a quarry of emotions, didn't want to eat.

Not to eat was not okay. Sister Evelyn stood over him with a spoonful of mashed potatoes demanding, "Put it in your mouth." She jabbed the spoon toward his mouth. Bud sniveled. A scream formed inside my empty chest, red and jagged. I was too scared to intervene. I swallowed. The unsounded scream cut my throat. The entire refectory population seemed to be focused on the little drama. Bud finally brought the contest to an end by throwing up in his plate. In a way, he'd won! Maybe that's why Sister Evelyn whipped him so often.

That night I again fell quickly to sleep. The next morning I met Jane Raynor, the girl in the alcove next to mine. I knew the nuns had told the other boarders about the motherless newcomers because, before she pulled the privacy curtains to dress, Jane whispered," When did your mother die?"

"Yesterday."

It seemed like yesterday. It seemed like a hundred years ago.

Lois and I didn't pull the curtain between our alcoves. Without my sister's familiar face, I was afraid I'd spin into space and be lost forever.

Boarding school life seemed a matter of bells and lines: chapel, refectory, classroom, jobs, study hall, dormitory. I joined the lines like someone joining line dances without knowing the steps. I seemed to be watching myself from a distance. I saw myself kneeling in chapel with a hankie bobby-pinned on my head, for example, or myself squaring the corners of my bed sheets.

Besides dividing me into the observer and the observed, homesickness hollowed me out. No one could see that the body called Eddie Mae was as empty as sky.

One day at recess, I was watching my empty self swing across the jungle gym bars with Jane Raynor when a 5th grade boy said, "Your dress is torn."

Jane Raynor—who seemed not afraid of anyone, not even a 5th grader—turned on him. "Shut up! Her mother just died."

Her retort made no sense at all, but it filled me with pity for the motherless girl crouched in a corner of the playground. I watched the girl sob and sob. During that recess period, my observing self joined my self observed.

With the sharp edges of loneliness softened by tears I felt more keenly a thick sludge of anger move inside the emptiness I had carried in my chest. Anger toward my mother for dying and my father for leaving us and Sister Evelyn for whipping my brother. My intense dislike of Sister Evelyn might have been partly inspired by a splitting-off of anger at my loss.

Partly, though, it flowed from her unfair bullying of the most defenseless boarders—Bud and some kids from the orphanage. It was as if Life, like a mother bird, had commanded us to fly and Bud could only flutter. My face grew hot with the realization that I had failed as caretaker of my brother and sister.

Years later, I worked a lot with children who'd lost a parent. They suffered from what could be called a child's version of traumatic stress. For a child, grief-work nearly always requires expressing rage and forgiving oneself. The process can take years. Long after the world has moved on, the child may be slowly, invisibly grieving.

After my playground tears and my shame at being an inadequate caretaker, I attempted to do a better job of living up to my big-sister responsibilities. I began by trying to curl Lois's hair like Mother had done.

> Neither of us suspected malignant
> cells were already nibbling
> away like termites at the floor
> of Mother's life on those school mornings
> when she'd summon you to the toasty kitchen
> to do your hair. I'd come, too,
> perch on a stool, sipping a cup of Ovaltine,
> aware that my own mop sat in Indian rebellion.
> I memorized the ritual—how Mother's
> fingers lingered as if reluctant to leave
> your black curls "like Shirley Temple's
> except for color" she'd say.
> I packed that memory and took it
> to the boarding school where,
> beside rows of lavatories in the dormitory's
> common bathroom, I wound your hair
> into clumsy spirals, fingers spelling *Mother*
> as if curls were a sign language that
> could bring her back to us. I couldn't
> successfully execute the ritual. But, Lois,
> remember this: I tried to curl your silk
> hair and wore my own like a warrior's.

Learning the politics of boarding-school life was tough. I discovered that there were three classes of boarders: those who paid tuition in full, those who worked off part of the tuition, and those from the orphanage.

Upper class, middle, and lower. As rule, the boarders paid scant attention to the day scholars. They were like aliens who arrived on school days and then vanished. Among the boarders, there were laws, most of them tacit.

I soon found out there were boarding-school bullies, too. I was lonely and desperate for a friend who could help me find my way through the maze of everything new. Rita seemed a likely candidate. Like me, she worked in the kitchen; we peeled potatoes together; we both sat in Sister Josepha's 3rd, 4th and 5th grade classroom, the only boarders in a class of eight; we slept two beds apart in the dormitory. Rita knew the ropes. I sought her friendship. But Rita was an emotional bully. Part of the skill of that brand of bullying, I learned, lay in dispensing friendliness in small doses then pulling it away. Other techniques used by Rita: freeze, sneers, sarcasm, shaming, indirection. I made a perfect victim.

Rita, I made 95 on the spelling test."

"So?"

Or silence.

Rita often used indirection. "Some people go around bragging about every little ol' grade." She would make comments like that, not to me, but to the boarders at the refectory table. As if I were a plate.

When the server placed a glass of cold milk beside my supper plate— my father paid $3 a month for us to have milk—Rita would say, "I wish some one would pay for me to have milk. It must be nice. But I don't pretend to be rich like some people I know."

Comments like this filled me with a sense of guilt. Or was it shame? I'd shove my glass of milk toward Rita, saying I didn't really want it. She never acknowledged the glass of milk. But she drank it.

Rita's harshest bullying technique was the "freeze." She wouldn't speak to me sometimes for days even as we stood elbow to elbow peeling potatoes in the kitchen. I'd try to make conversation. I might make a comment about school. Silence. I might mention that the potatoes had lots of eyes. Silence. I'd try a direct question. "Did you write anything on the card for Sister Josepha's feast day?" Silence. Six potatoes later I'd try again. "Have you memorized the poem for tomorrow yet?" Silence.

Then one day, Rita would say something like, "Want to play on the slide?" That was my reward—a teaspoon of friendliness.

Nothing in Blue Heaven or in the pipe yard had taught me how to cope with that kind of subtle meanness. I tended to blame myself. What had I done to make her mad? Oh, the stomach ache!

Between Rita's bullying and my concern for Bud, I was miserable. I don't know why Rita's approval of me was so important. She couldn't replace my mother, my father, my home. Partly because I thought I couldn't survive without Rita's friendship, I stuffed my feelings of loss. But grief waited. It always does.

It was my little sister who forced me to challenge what I call emotional bullying. "You let Rita lead you around by the nose." What she meant, the message I understood, was, "Get some backbone."

My fear of Rita's rejection was not as strong as my need for Lois's approval. Without cohesion, our fragment of family would die. The breakthrough came at supper. I
drank my own milk. Noisily! "Boy, is this good." I spoke to the table, not to Rita.

Bullies seem to sense their victim's weakness or strength. Hitting, punching, pinching bullies are easily detectable. Emotional bullies—those who practice almost invisibly on those without psychological resources—can be unseen.

Jane Raynor became a lifelong friend. She belonged to the minority whose folks paid full tuition, and I belonged to the group of those who worked. Boarding-school unspoken rules dictated adherence to one's own group, so becoming friends with a full-payer was not a politically correct thing to do. But by then, I'd been toughened enough to disregard those rules. Being a year younger than me and a year older than Lois, Jane became a kind of link that enabled me to stay close to my sister. Lois's face remained my compass. Several years later, Jane would sneak out of the dormitory with Lois and me to catch a midnight train with plans to live large and free.

Jane had freckles and a nose made pug by her habit of wiping it with an upward swipe of her hand. In bits and pieces, Jane's story took form. She'd been an unwelcome surprise to her well-off parents who didn't seem to mind shelling out money as long as she left them alone. Even as a child, I figured she was worse off than most of us. She became like a sister to Lois and me.

A letter came from Daddy. "Dear Babies, How are you? I am just fine. Am in California picking oranges. Will send you a box of oranges. Love, Daddy." The letter brought a surge of sickening longing. We read and re-read the letter as if the sheet of paper were a ship come to rescue three kids stranded on an island. When the oranges arrived we handed them out like balls of sunshine. They were sweet with thick-rinds.

I loved working in the kitchen. Sister Brigid, the cook, found a box for me to stand on so I could reach and peel potatoes. The boarders ate a five-gallon bucket of potatoes every day. Sister Brigid's false teeth constantly clicked. She would never see her home again. She had grown up in Ireland and at least twice she lifted her habit a few inches above small feet and tried to teach me an Irish jig.

Once Sister Brigid told me—with watery eyes and clicking teeth—that when she had joined the order, she'd thought it would be a life of prayer, not kitchen duty that kept her in the basement kitchen while the other Sisters were upstairs in chapel. It wasn't like her to confide something so personal. I think she thought I'd understand. In a way, I did because, in a way, I loved her. Sister Brigid was a kind of surrogate mother.

Christmas vacation came. Parents came to take their children home. But when Joanna called from the front porch, "Sister Geraline wants the three Tate kids in her office," it was not our father who had come to get us but his oldest sister, our Aunt Rachel. Aunt Rachel and the rest of the Nelson family lived in Oklahoma City on Northwest 29th Street. We thought the Nelsons were rich because their house was brick. Aunt Rachel and Uncle Fergus had a daughter, our cousin, Wanda. Their son had been a test pilot but was killed in a plane accident.

The Nelson house felt tense. Wanda scowled. Uncle Fergus coughed. Aunt Rachel made us use our napkins. Wanda's voice was thin and nasal. It reminded me of the sound made by a handful of gravel thrown against a tin shed. One day, Lois overheard Wanda ask Aunt Rachel how long "the Tate brats" would be there.

According to a story my father had told, Wanda didn't like her mother. "The problem was that they both loved the same man," is the way my father put it. Poor Uncle Fergus. Evidently Wanda blamed her mother, the other woman in the strange triangle, when Uncle Fergus made clear that loyalty to wife ranked above defense of daughter. My father told the story this way:

Years earlier, Wanda had fallen in love with a young man—family lore doesn't name the fiancé—and had brought him home to meet her folks. During the meal, she'd said, "Shut up" to her prattling mother at which point Uncle Fergus reached across the table and slapped her for the insolence. Wanda fled the table in loud, hacking tears. "Shortly after this glimpse into the beatitude of family life," my father loved this part and I memorized it verbatim, "the fiancé broke the engagement and Wanda grew into a bitter career woman working at the Oklahoma City Chamber of Commerce." The story may or may not be true. My father was not loath to improve a story by adding a bit of drama. Factual or not, Wanda clearly disliked her mother. She appeared to love only her dad and her Chihuahuas, Tommy and Timmy.

In the past, the story had created in me a kind of ungenerous glee at the fate of Wanda, but being in the Nelson home and witnessing the family interactions caused in me a fuzzy envy. At least the Nelsons were a unit with family stories, family secrets, an ongoing history, even love, flawed as love seems wont to be.

Sometimes after Wanda had driven off to work and the house exhaled, Aunt Rachel sat down at the piano and played "Cherokee (Indian Love Song)". Your love keeps calling/ my heart enthralling/ Oooh, Cherokee. I remember sitting on the floor in her bedroom and weeping. What is it about music that breaks and breaks the heart! Not the voice. My aunt had a rusty-wire voice. Nor was it the felt hammers striking the strings. It was the sound aching with the oooh? Oooh was, after all, a non-word. Like tears. Even back then, I understood in a half-lit way that sorrow cannot be translated. I couldn't have said why I loved the mornings Aunt Rachel played the "Indian Love Song."

I have to admire my aunt for taking us home with her in the face of Wanda's disapproval. Things became especially tense when my aunt decided we needed "a good cleaning out" and set the project in motion with little pink pills. Wanda didn't like those "scrawny kids stinking up the only bathroom."

I was almost relieved when Aunt Rachel put us—squeaky clean intestines and all—into the Pontiac and headed south to Chickasha and Jane. Good, comfortable Jane. She'd gone to her married sister's house for Christmas dinner. Her parents had been there, too.

On January 9, 1937, I was on the playground teeter-tottering, when Rita came outside shouting, "Sister Geraline wants to see the Tate kids in her office." This time there was no Christmas vacation to imagine. I ran up the stairs examining my conscience.

And there stood Daddy!

We pushed past Sister Geraline, squealing. Bud began to sob. Daddy picked him up. Bud sobbed wetly on our father's shoulder. "Oh, Daddy, Daddy." I heard a sound about to happen in Daddy's chest. I tightened. But the sound didn't come. "It's okay, little man," my husky-voiced father said, "You're coming home with me."

"Are you sure this is wise, Mr. Tate?"

Daddy nodded and picked up his fedora.

"They've only been here three months," Sister Geraline reminded him. "They've already been in two schools this year."

"They're all I've got, Sister. I'll take them home with me."

"Home" was a house between the little towns of Sacred Heart—already on its way to becoming a ghost town—and Konawa. The dream I'd had of the house erased from the pipe yard in Oklahoma City had been accurate.

The house Daddy took us to was better than any we'd so far lived in. We walked through it like tourists. Like the Blue Heaven houses, it was clapboard, but it was roomier—a large kitchen, a bedroom for Lois and me and a second bedroom for Daddy and Bud. We even had a living room with a sofa, a rocking chair, and a little table on which Daddy'd placed Mother's scrapbook and a clock. He had bought and hung curtains patterned with big roses. I think we were all intimidated by such a formal room. Most of the time, we shied away from it.

The owner of the oil company had arranged for Daddy to maintain several pumps. Flexible pipes slid back and forth over the ground connecting outlying wells to the main engine house. If the new job as pumper seemed boring to my father after a dozen years working on the drilling-end of oil wells, he never let us know. What he did let us know was his joy in having us near. He bought a milk cow. He built a screened-in porch. He hired Mr. Johnson to help plant an acre or two of alfalfa. When I hear the word green today, I think alfalfa.

Big oil tanks squatted like fat toads in our new home's yard. Metal steps crawled up their sides. Of course we climbed the steps and dipped the long measuring rods into the tanks. An unused derrick still stood close to an old slush pit. Sometimes the scene was transformed to beautiful. "Come see the sunset," Daddy would call. "Oklahoma has the prettiest sunsets in the country." To my father even the slush pit became part poem, part fairy tale.

> It began when the setting sun transformed the pit
> to glass reflecting a world we couldn't see
> in daylight: a blue-pink-violet scarf
> of sky, the derrick a silver lattice. The pump
> continued to dip-and-lift. The drowned cat
> became a lump of gold. A hawk spread wings
> in two unearthly worlds at once—in sky
> and deep within the sunset's mirrored pit.
>
> It was as if beneath the surface lay
> a memory of where we'd come from and where we'd go.
> At those evening dreaming times, we exchanged
> experience for wonder and stood in diaphanous awe.
> The shine reminded us that inside our froggy skin
> we're really royalty waiting to be kissed again.

Many times my father fell into a kind of Indian poetry. Once he showed me tiny blue wild flowers half-hidden in the alfalfa field. "Chips of Father Sky. Father Sky," he said. He called the fireflies that lit their lanterns at dusk, "little sisters,"—an Indian version of St. Francis of Assisi.

My father's mother had been half Choctaw and kept to the Old Ways. As a child, my father had been sent to the Indian Boarding School in Chilocco, an Oklahoma town close to the Kansas border. He had been an unwilling student. He told me that every night he curled around an ache "big and ugly as a mangy dog shivering in my chest."

At the Chilocco school, my father had learned to read. He'd also learned to wear knickers and white boys' shoes—"not as comfy as moccasins, not by a long shot." When his half-Choctaw mother visited him in the Chilocco parlor, she seemed shy around her son. "She treated me like a stranger," he said, shaking his head. But he had learned to read, and he read a lot.

The school at Chilocco, two stories high with tall windows, was among the first Indian Boarding School built after the 1882 Congress authorized their construction. When my father went there, light spilled from the tall windows across the grassland and earned the school the nickname, "Light of the Prairie."

Government Indian schools were run like military base camps—which stands to reason since they were modeled after a school experiment devised by Captain Richard Pratt in a military prison. Captain Pratt's educational philosophy, "Kill the Indian, save the man" was adopted by the schools. The intention of the schools was to extinguish Indian culture and help Indians assimilate into the general culture. To that end, students were taught to read, write, and practice Christianity. Girls had lessons in cleaning, sewing, and doing laundry. Servant work. Boys were taught to farm and build. During the summers, students lived with white families instead of returning to their homes. That system—called "outing"—made relapse into Indian ways less likely.

Daddy enrolled us in St. Mary's Academy close to what was left of Sacred Heart Abbey, the original Benedictine Monastery now located in Shawnee. In 1880, five Sisters had come to Indian Territory and begun St. Mary's Academy which served both day students and boarders. Most of the day students at St. Mary's Academy were from nearby German farm families. Most boarding students were members of the Potawatomi or other Indian tribes. Indian students were forbidden to speak their native language. That rule, of course, was useless. Sister Francesca carried an Indian/English dictionary in her pocket. It, too, was useless. I found the Indian students exotic. In fact, I promised God I'd name my first daughter after a willowy girl name Mahonna. I'm not sure why I thought God cared. I remember chanting, "Ma hon na" on the way home from school. The name sparkled like flowing water.

During recess at St. Mary's, I sometimes slipped through a grove of trees to the site of the old monastery. A few wizened nuns still lived there. They wore a habit I hadn't seen before. Little could I have guessed that someday I'd wear the same strange garb. Those nuns spoke rapid-fire French. Language was all they had left of the country they'd left in 1875. Until the 1901 monastery fire, those French women had cooked and cleaned for both the monks and the Indian boys enrolled in the monastery's Industrial School.

When I sneaked off the school grounds and went to where the monastery had stood, I had no way of knowing I was glimpsing the ruins of a dramatic past. But even as a child, I sensed a passing of history.

Sacred Heart Monastery was a good example of the so-called butterfly effect. In this case, the phenomenon applied not to the hypothetical butterfly in Brazil that causes a hurricane in Texas but to anticlerical laws in France that caused a monks to build a monastery in Oklahoma. If France had not become so anti-clerical in the 1880s, French priests probably would not have left their country and headed out for far-away Oklahoma Territory. On land given by the Potawatomi tribe, the tough monks from France slept in tents, rose to pray in the dark, ate very little—bread and three prunes for supper—and outworked even the German homesteaders who had settled around there. Even though the monks stopped working several times a days to pray, they managed to build a monastery, plant orchards and crops, and operate an Industrial School for Indian boys. In 1901 fire destroyed everything except the stone bakery. By that time, American monks outnumbered the Frenchmen who'd come to Indian Territory. The Americans adopted a less austere type of Benedictine life and, instead of rebuilding on the original site, they moved to Shawnee where they built Saint Gregory's Monastery.

A few years ago, a friend and I took a nostalgic trip back to the site of the monastery and the school we had attended in the 30s. The buildings of both institutions have burned to the ground.

> Indeed, all that remains of the monastery
> are a stone bakery and two cemeteries,
> one for the monks and farther back, partially
> veiled by cedar trees, one for the nuns
>
> who'd sailed from France and ridden
> constipating stagecoach for days,
> come to clean and bake bread for the hairy
> half-cowboy half-missionary men.
>
> Monastery archives mention the nuns
> just enough to document
> that they came, cooked, died
> and were buried here where nobody comes

anymore except grasshoppers,
the straw-hatted man bumping across graves
on his John Deere mower,
and, today, my friend and me.

Lichen has eaten into the brief biographies
scratched on sandstone markers, leaving
neither name nor age above whatever's left
of old-women's bones in pine boxes.

My friend and I walked over to the site of the academy that Lois, Bud, and I had attended. Nothing remains except a metal arch knee-deep in Johnston grass.

The Tates may have been the only unchurched family attending St. Mary's Academy. We were not atheists, not even agnostics. We could be called the know-nothings. Of course that didn't excuse us from catechism classes. Three months at St. Joseph's Boarding School in Chickasha had taught me the routine. Students stood along the wall spelling-bee fashion; Sister asked catechism questions and we spouted answers. If a student didn't know an answer—a rare occurrence—a sternly disappointed nun ordered, "Take your seat." It was a humiliation. I never had to sit down. I loved catechism. Just think, the thorniest questions had concise answers. Question: Why did my mother die? Answer: She didn't die; she lives on free of pain and happy in heaven. I didn't ask, Why does missing her still feel like a hole inside me?

The four of us settled into a life almost idyllic. Daddy usually had supper ready for us when we came home from school. He set the table and nearly every afternoon, we found one or all of the dishes upside down. Under a plate or cup we'd find a piece of candy and feign surprise. "Ooh, look! Mine's cherry." "Mine's grape." Daddy beamed.

Most Saturdays, we went into Konawa to go to the picture show. Double feature. We usually stayed the entire afternoon. While we twice watched Gene Autry rescue a Western town from thugs or twice watched Flash Gordon and the lovely Dale Arden rid planets of unfriendly aliens, Daddy played poker or pitch in the pool hall next door. Flash Gordon movies were serial and typically ended in an explosion or some other can-he-escape-this episode, so we thought we had to go the following Saturday. That was fine with Daddy.

Etta Mae Ingram, a neighbor our age, had never been to a picture show, so one Saturday we invited her to go with us. It wasn't fun. She ducked under the seat to avoid being hit by a stray bullet from Tonto's gun.

Sometimes Daddy gathered poke which he boiled with fatback. Once he served calf brain. Only once. He milked Bossie and filled our glasses with cold milk. We had a water pump but the water tasted like iron, so every day Daddy drove to Konawa with a milk can wired to the car's front bumper to get fresh water and a block of ice for the refrigerator. That's where he was the day the house caught fire.

The fire must have started in the storeroom which was situated behind the kitchen directly opposite the cook stove. A drought had lasted four months. Oklahoma sun had siphoned every drop of moisture from every sunflower and leaf. Our house was tinder. Daddy had gone to Konawa to get water. I noticed smoke curling under the storeroom door. Then flames. Lois's violin was in there, but when I tried to get it, heat and smoke knocked me back. "Here," I said with big-sisterly wisdom, handing a water dipper to Lois, "you and Bud put it out with water. I'll go get Mrs. Ingram."

I ran across the cotton field. Mrs. Ingram was churning, the wooden plunger going up/ down/ up/ down.

"Miss Ingram!" I was out of breath. "Miss Ingram, our house is on fire."

She dropped the churn paddle and ran out into the dirt yard, shading her eyes against the afternoon's merciless glare. I turned around to see flames licking the roof of our house. I felt sick. Dear God! I'd left my sister and brother inside ladling dippers of water. In a kind of awful slow motion, the roof folded and sank. My knees gave out and I sat down on the step to keep from falling. I was supposed to take care of them. Now I had let them burn to death!

When Lois and Bud ran panting into the Ingrams' dirt yard, I began to cry. Thank God, they'd disobeyed me.

Bud pointed. "Look! There's Daddy!"

We squinted at the dirt road a half mile away where Daddy's car bounced in a cloud of red dust toward the inferno. Even the car looked panicked.

The nuns at St. Mary's let us stay with the boarders until the oil-company owner sent a truck with another house. The replacement was a shotgun house, uglier than most. The ceiling sagged. The walls were water-stained. The truck drivers who had brought the house, had placed it in a patch of weeds and perched it on cement blocks in such as way that anyone driving up could easily see under it from side to side, front to back. It felt precarious. Never more so than when a tornado came, as tornadoes are wont to do in Oklahoma, especially in spring.

> Maybe it was the lilt of el or the lingering *ar*
> or maybe the *oo* that moans in every language
> that caused non-English speakers surveyed
> by Associated Press to choose *cellar door* as
> the most beautiful sound in English. To me,
> the words conjure the Johnson's shovel-dug
> haven with its heavy oak-and-iron door.
> When tornadoes threatened to lower ropy
> vacuums into Konawa, OK. Daddy piled us
> three kids into the Chevy and battled four
> miles of bucking wind to Johnsons' cellar.
>
> When Mr. Johnson lit the kerosene lantern and set it
> atop the barrel of blackberries turning into wine,
> eerie shapes flickered to life on the cellar's mud
> walls, and bloodless spiders rappelled from rafters
> like blind ghosts gliding into the knee-level shadows.
> When wind rattled the cellar door and banged
> its iron handle, we grew goose bumpy and circled
> closer around Mr. Johnson's lantern's meager fire.

Back home one gray day after a trip to the cellar, I stood at the sink, in the dingy kitchen washing dishes. It was raining. Daddy was at the kitchen table. I began to weep.

"What's the matter, Baby?" I didn't know.

Aunt Rachel used to play "Pennies from Heaven" on the piano. "And you shouldn't be afraid for / Every time it rains, it rains / Pennies from heaven." I didn't believe those words.

Tears seemed to come easily in that run-down house. Once Daddy surprised me with his. We were in the kitchen again.

"What's the matter, Daddy?"

"The way you turned your head just now," he said. "Like your mother used to do." He buried his face in his hands. "I miss her. Oh, God, I miss her." That was the first time I glimpsed my father's aching loneliness. I didn't know that he, too, grieved. I was nine years old; what did I know of a man's loss?

If the world we live in shapes us—and I believe it does—the house itself became a sadness holding a sad family. My emotional landscape seemed as leaky and shabby as the house. It was as if the shabbiness I lived in had penetrated my skin and settled in my psyche. I carried shabbiness to school.

In keeping with our scant lives, Daddy bought a little canvas-and-tin contraption and began to roll his own cigarettes. He opened the Bull Durham pouch—always handy in his shirt pocket—and shook tobacco into a thin filter paper, turned the handle which wound a canvas belt and rolled the filter paper around the tobacco, and presto! a wobbly cigarette with empty ends which, when lit, caused a conflagration that threatened to set fire to the smoker's eyebrows.

During this period I decided we should all be baptized so we could go to heaven. St. Benedict's parish church smelled musty but it was clean and beautiful. When I knelt in church, I tried to inhale the antique beauty. Maybe sacramental water would wash away not only sin from my soul but also sordidness from my sense of self.

I had to adjust my plans down from four baptisms to three. My father would have nothing to do with it, saying he didn't think God was a Catholic. "Besides," he said, "I've been a pretty good Indian." But he had no objection to our becoming Catholic. "It might not help you, but it sure as hell can't hurt."

With that dubious blessing, I approached Father Basil before Sunday Mass with my request. I suppose he considered attendance at St. Mary's Academy instruction enough. In 1937 the selection of godparents was a casual affair, indeed. So, at the end of Mass, red-haired Father Basil announced to the congregation, "The Tate kids are going to be baptized. I need someone to be godparents. Who'll stand up for the first one? That'll be Eddie Mae." The Kissenstaffers—Kurstenstaffers?—stood up for me. I don't remember the godparents for Lois and Bud.

One day in June, Aunt Rachel steered her Pontiac through the weeds to our house. The big, polished car looked as out of place as Flash Gordon's space ship would've. With a sweeping glance, she took in the sagging ceilings, torn linoleum, cramped rooms, and our chigger-bitten legs. She and my father had a long conversation out of earshot—which means they went outside. When they returned, my father looked stooped. Maybe he had simply stopped being young.

Aunt Rachel kissed us goodbye in a cloud of scent: Lady Ester Face Powder and Pond's Face Cream. Daddy walked her to her car. As she arranged herself at the steering wheel, she said, "Remember, Ed, it's best for them. This" a dismissive gesture that included the house, privy, weeds, oil tanks, " is no place to raise your girls. Look at them; they look like wild Indians."

"I know, Rachel. I know." He was a defeated man.

On the way back to St. Joseph's Boarding School in Chickasha, our father was silent. Bud rolled his body into a circle in the back seat—the o of no. He, too, was silent.

Even before Sister Geraline ushered us into the room with the glossy floor, the blend of clean smells caused a shift inside me. Something tightened. A bed was made. Floor wax, laundry bleach, candles, old books. Lonely odors that left me feeling simultaneously comforted and abandoned. Even today, the smell of floor wax whisks me back to the parlor where Daddy left us. Once I broke into public tears in a bank with a shiny floor.

Bud returned to porch duty and, in dread, to Sister Evelyn. Lois continued to clean the music rooms. Returning to the kitchen and the unvarying bucket of potatoes felt safe to me. Sister Brigid—false teeth still clicking—took me back under her wide black wing.

Besides kitchen duty, I was also assigned to help with the laundry.

The boarding-school laundry room
is all steam and scorch. White shirts,
sprinkled and rolled tight as secrets,
wait in a basket at my ironing board.

It's my job between class dismissal
and supper, supper and Study Hall,
to press the shirts. I spit on a finger
and test the sizzle of a flat iron.
Begin with the collar, Sister Evelyn
reminds me. Keep the iron moving.

Forth and back, over and over. I fall
into every Tuesday's white trance—
any snowy thing possible:
souls after absolution,
seven-minute frosting,
angels bearing me away. Away.

Years slid off the calendar steady as peelings from potatoes: 1938.
1939. 1940. 1941. 1942. 1943.

Bud shrank into himself. Lois became studious and pious. I read. We
made friends. Like children everywhere, we found ways to adjust and
survive.

We didn't see Daddy much. He was, by nature, nomadic. A Plains
Indian at heart. He carried his loss across America like a blanket. He
occasionally wrote us, always in pencil on tablet paper, always the same
letter except for location and job: "Dear Babies, How are you? I am just
fine. I miss you a lot. Am in [choose one: a. Mexico picking cotton, b.
Kansas shucking corn, c. Canada harvesting wheat.] Love, Your Dad."

The best thing about being in the 6th grade was Sister Amadeus. The
next best thing was the cloak room—a large window-lit room which,
besides hooks for coats and three tall shelves for classroom supplies, also
housed a bookcase. That was our classroom library. So handy. When Sister
Amadeus focused her attention to the two middle rows where the 7th
graders sat in the three-grade classroom, I slipped into the cloak room.
There I sat cross-legged on the floor, tuned an ear to our teacher's voice so
I could return to my seat in time for 6th grade lessons, and read. I began

with the first book on the top shelf. I was indiscriminate in my reading. The preposterous lives of the saints, Little Women, the Tom Swift books, all the Elsie Dinsmore stories. Elsie's mother had died, too.

By the time I reached the middle of the 7th grade, I'd read my way to the encyclopedias on the bottom shelf. What a treasure trove. I must have been so engrossed in the mystery of the digestive system (Volume D) that I didn't hear the clink of Sister Amadeus's rosary beads which always preceded the nuns like the "odor of sanctity" the saints typically died in. I was deep inside the small intestine when a pale hand from the outside world gently lifted the book, closed it, and handed it back. "Put this where it belongs, Eddie Mae, and come to your seat. It's time for 7th grade Geography." No scolding. I loved Sister Amadeus.

In fact, I loved school. It was a predictable world. Facts, figures, and each part of speech had its proper place. Yes, and order. First, the oceans, then continents, then nations. Diagramming sentences became an art. A complex-compound sentence could take up half a sheet of notebook paper —straight lines, slanted lines, words on stilts, phrases dangling.

Sister Amadeus read to us. Stories, poems, essays. We scanned and memorized poetry. The poem I most clearly remember is "Opportunity" by Edward Sill. "There spread a cloud of dust along a plain"—pure iambic pentameter. We learned the various kinds of rhyme: masculine and feminine and their unpopular cousins, slant and near. Unfortunately, though, poetry was less art than life-lesson. We mined each poem for its application to us. This, for instance, from "Opportunity":   No complaining. Life handed you a dull sword? Use it.

Every six weeks the boarders assembled to receive their report cards from Sister Geraline. She named a student, scanned the grades, and presented the card with a public commentary. It was a powerful motivation. Lois always made straight A's "Good work." Lois would walk back to her seat flushed with the praise. I was proud of her. When it was my turn, Sister Geraline squinched her face and sighed, "Why can't you be more like your sister?"

I continued to frequent the cloak room because Sister Amadeus hadn't frowned when she called me a "book worm." Someone had inserted into the encyclopedia (S-Volume) a carbon-copy of a typed report of the WPA's interviews of former slaves in Oklahoma. It was my first exposure to dialect: *Marse Tom been dead a long time. I s'pect he's in hell. Seem lak dat where he 'long.*

The day I read about oysters in the O-Volume, I sat on the cloakroom floor weeping. I couldn't have said why. The ocean was so enormous. The hatchlings were so tiny. They were on their own to find a place to cling. A big fish could eat them, and who would know? Or care?

When Bud died a few months ago, I thought of that day.

> If I could write my brother's obituary
>
> I'd write about oysters.
> Sent to fend for themselves in the battering ocean,
>   oyster larvae look for something, anything to cling to.
> Like you, cast young into the beating boarding school sea,
>   an eat-or-be-eaten world. You learned to eat.
> When oysters lose footing, they drift seeking another home.
>   In the army you learned to shoot or be shot.
> One zero-degree day you gathered into the steel basket of his
>   helmet bits of shrapnel and your tent-mate's brain.
> When an oyster ingests something sharp, it coats the pain
>   over and over again with nacre.
> Sometimes the resulting pearl is black.
>   Always it's iridescent.

Bud was in the second grade when Daddy took us back to St. Joseph's. But, while I could pinpoint the day my observing self joined my self observed, he still seemed to be ungrounded. He was probably seven years old the day he ran wide-eyed to me on the playground wailing, "I think she killed me." He meant it. He was that unattached to himself. I followed him to the boys' dorm where he showed me the evidence: bloody sheets. I lifted the pillow and found his loose-capped bottle of shoe polish. "Oxblood Brown." What should a big sister do in such a circumstance? This big sister stole a clean pillow and bottom sheet from two beds over. If someone years later found a stained mattress, well, presumably we'd be gone. "Go on out and play," I advised my still-frightened brother. Shortly after the shoe polish incident, Sister Brigid began telling me about Hitler. "The Nazis," she said, eyes watering, "skin the Jews and make lamp shades."

Slaves. Oysters. Bud. The Jews. Was no one safe? Where were the protectors?

Daddy came for my eighth-grade graduation. He wore his suit. He took us to a photography studio for a family picture, then to a shop where he bought me a new dress. I sulked. I couldn't snap out of my big pout. I felt trapped inside myself. When I tried on the dress, Daddy said, "You look pretty." "Thanks." It literally hurt my throat to talk. "Pink's a good color for you." "Thanks." "Your mother liked pink. It was her favorite color." An image of sweet peas flashed into my mind and tightened my already tight throat. I said nothing. Daddy looked at me quizzically. Oh, if only I could break out of myself. I couldn't. After he left, angry longing lay in my throat like a lodged rock. Flinty. Begging for tears.

I entered adolescence. In the girls' dormitory, we opened curtains between alcoves and compared legs, lifting them like Marlene Dietrich. I had good legs. Boobs were important, too. Lola Mae, 36C, was the champion. I stuffed my A cups with hankies.

Decades later, researching the meaning of clothes and body shapes, I would learn that when a country loses men and women in war and therefore needs to replenish its population, women's styles emphasize the nurturing breasts. Lola Mae was ahead of her time. I fretted about my flat chest and late start of menstruation. It almost seemed unpatriotic.

It was Sister Evelyn who introduced me to the mystery of the sanitary belt, a tangle of elastic. Matter-of-factly she showed me how to attach a Kotex.

"You're lucky," she said. "When I started, we used rags." I was shocked. Nuns menstruated?

During the summer vacation months, the teaching nuns pitched in to help Sister Evelyn watch over the boarders who stayed in the boarding school. Sister Amadeus took us to the park. Once or twice Sister Brigid packed a picnic for us. Occasionally Sister Maurita lined us up and took us into town to a movie approved by The Legion of Decency: The Wizard of Oz, Mr. Smith Goes to Washington, Goodbye, Mr. Chips. Jane and I would have liked to see Gone with the Wind. And Sister Evelyn eased up on us either because her work load was shared or because she wanted the other Sisters to see her on good behavior. Whatever the reason, we enjoyed the reprieve.

Aunt Rachel continued to take us to her house for a few days every Christmas and for a week during the summer. During the summer visit, we could count on a trip downtown to Brown's Department Store. We usually headed for bargains in the basement where our aunt purchased the clothes we'd need for the coming year.

We didn't like going to the Nelsons' house, but we liked our aunt. She had reared her kids and now she was helping her brother rear his. She mended, threw away what we'd outgrown, and looked for underwear bargains. We didn't mind the clothes routine but dreaded the good "cleaning out" she insisted that we needed. Daddy did his part by paying her and by paying not only tuition and milk but also for the piano lessons she insisted we have. We missed Daddy. We wished Aunt Rachel would tell him to come see us more often.

We continued to feel awkward around Wanda. When Timmy and Tommy barkedwild greetings at her arrival home from work, all three of us became the gawky tongue-tied cousins she expected us to be. The only time I remember being spontaneous in the presence of Wanda was the day she beat a stray cat to death.

It had been a hotter-than-usual August day. Uncle Fergus was out of town. We were fanning ourselves in the Nelsons' backyard, a space made precisely square by a dense well-trimmed hedge. Except for the times she baby-talked to Timmy and Tommy, Wanda wore the silent scowl we'd grown used to. For the most part, silence held us in an awkward embrace; so I literally jumped when Wanda suddenly, exclaimed, "Git! Git out." The Chihuahuas had commenced a series of yips, whines, and tinny growls. A skinny cat dashed back through the hedge to the alley. But evidently finding the smell of food stronger than fear, it nosed forward again. This time, when the dogs advanced, the cat arched its back and hissed. That did it. Wanda grabbed a hoe and gave chase. It was almost comical to see our straddle-legged cousin diving right and left to block the cat's escape through the hedge. Eventually she trapped the hissing animal in the garage. "Eddie Mae," she shouted—I hadn't been sure she knew my name—"shut the door." I ran to the garage but stopped at the entrance. The cat was cowering in a corner.

Wanda was chopping at it with the hoe. Thin quirts of blood followed each chop. "Stop," I screamed. "No. No. Stop it." Finally the damaged cat leaked past her legs into the yard. Wanda ran after it. "Shut up, Eddie Mae," she yelled at me over her shoulder. I must have been screaming. "I told you to close the door." The cat collapsed in the middle of the yard. The dogs circled it, sniffing. Wanda lifted the limp carcass with a hankie and dropped it in the garbage can.

"Mangy thing. That'll teach you to scare my dogs."
Aunt Rachel acted as if nothing had happened. Lois and Bud could have been stones. I sat in my chair, heart pounding, nose running. My throat was plugged with screams. I hated my cousin.

In the ninth grade, I lost my faith in Catechism answers. I blame—or credit—a priest.

It happened the day Monsignor Monaghan, superintendent of Catholic schools, visited our classroom and asked us to tell him how we experienced God.

"Forget the catechism," he unbelievably said. "Use your imagination."
Imagination?

We were dumbstruck. Literally. Struck dumb. At the top of the blackboard, Sister Maurita had written in colored-chalk calligraphy a reminder that Speech is silver. Silence is golden. That day, the entire class chose golden. The good monsignor rolled his eyes. Then he told us about Francis Thompson, a sometimes-druggie living on London's dirty streets, who had written a long poem in which God starred as—of all things—a bloodhound. "You won't find that in a catechism," he said.

> He began reciting "The Hound of Heaven"
> his long shoes pacing the poem's cadence
> across the wood floor. There in our chalky classroom
> the monsignor with shiny shoes and red biretta
>
> forgot trim and tassel. He became simply a man,
> passionate, hoarse-voiced, declaring that everyone
> runs and the relentless Hound chases, chases after.
> I leaned spellbound into the rhythmic pursuit.
> That was the day, learning metaphor, I lost my faith
>
> in dogma. That was the day I converted to poetry—
> its precise imprecision, its beat, its heresy, its truth.

I'd never before been stung like that by poetry. And already I longed to be stung again.

That same year, 1940, Sister Brigid relayed more news about Nazi atrocities.

"They're killing Jews by the hundreds," she said, shaking her head. "They stack the dead bodies like firewood and burn them in big ovens."

I tried to imagine the horror. I thought of the dead cat. No catechism could answer Why? I wished for a metaphor.

"Eddie Mae, your brother wants you," Dale called. Bud was sitting on the ground behind the school. When I got there, he unbuckled his belt and inched his pants down just enough to show me a sausage-like bubble.

"Are my insides spilling out?"

"Nah." I was scared to death. "How did it happen?"

"I don't know. She got mad at me for sweeping the dirt behind the trash can." When it came to explaining, Bud always said more than he needed to. "She grabbed my broom and hit me with it." "She," of course, meant "Sister Evelyn."

I looked at the protrusion again. It was a problem I couldn't solve by stealing a bed sheet.

"Golly," I said wisely.

I didn't know the protrusion had a name. Hernia.

But right there on the spot, I knew what I had to do. "I'll go get a job and then I'll come back and get you and take you to a doctor."

He didn't trust me.

"How about Daddy? How about Aunt Rachel?"

"I don't know exactly where Daddy is, but when I get to Oklahoma City, I'll call Aunt Rachel. Don't worry. As soon as I get a job, I'll come back for you. I'll knock three times on the boys' dorm window." I'd read too many spy stories.

"Keep your belt over that bubble."

I persuaded Lois and Jane Raynor to go with me. The plot was laid. When Sister Evelyn left her keys on a table somewhere—as she had a habit of doing—I was to pick them up and open the candy cupboard where she kept the boarders' spending money. We estimated Jane's allowance plus ours to be $33.10.

As planned, Sister left the keys and I, sweaty-palmed, counted out the amount that matched our calculations.   No more.

Since I was to be the job-seeker, I needed to look sophisticated. That meant lots of red, red lipstick. At midnight, I applied the lipstick, donned one of Wanda's shortened dresses, stuffed my bra, and Voila! transformation. I thought I looked downright sophisticated. We sneaked out of the dormitory and carried our suitcases to the train station on South 6th Street. The tickets to Oklahoma City cost $11. A whopping third of the cash we had.

Everything went downhill after we got off the train in Oklahoma City. It was still dark. We had no lodging. The adrenalin had decreased and left us sleepy. Our cardboard suitcases were heavy. We were hungry so we bought a bottle of unpasteurized milk (19 cents) and day-old donuts (ten cents) and had what I tried to convince Lois and Jane was a "picnic" on the curb. Our cash supply was shrinking.

I led the way to a building with a faded sign, Rooms, and told the woman behind the desk we'd like to rent a one-bedroom room for one night.

"I don't rent by the night. This is a boarding house, dearie."

Dearie? With one word she stripped away my pretense of being the grownup in charge.

"I lease by the week--$20.00," she continued. "In advance." I opened my purse and handed over 20 one-dollar bills. I bought a newspaper. The purse was shrinking.

Lois, almost asleep, stood dangerously lopsided. What had she packed in that suitcase? The woman led us to a small room with one full-sized bed.

"Good grief!" Jane squealed after the woman closed the door. "Is that a cockroach?"

Lois put her suitcase down and flopped on the bed. A cloud of dust rose. We couldn't see out the windows. The sink was yellow. We remembered the woman's filthy apron. "Everything's dirty," Lois said. "You couldn't pay me to stay here."

So we picked up our suitcases and left, $20.00 poorer. But first we spread the want ads out on the unclean bed and searched for a job. A woman wanted a "Mexican girl" to clean her house for $50.00 a week plus lunch. We agreed I should apply. I found a telephone, placed a nickel, and dialed the number listed.

The ad-placer asked if I had experience. "Yes, lots." She asked my name.

"Ramona. Ramona Brown." The woman said Brown didn't sound Mexican. "It's my mother's name." Dumb. She didn't hire me.

Hungry, very tired, and still jobless, we carried our suitcases to a cemetery and sat down to think on a concrete bench beneath a concrete angel. And that's where three greasy-haired boys driving a greenish Studebaker found us.

"You girls look tired." The driver's bare arm hung out the window like a thick brown club.

I assured them we weren't tired. Lois and Jane assured them we were.

"Get in," said the owner of the hairy club. He reached back and opened the left rear door. "One of us for each of y'all."

Lois and Jane wanted to get in. I didn't trust the boys. They looked oily. Fear drummed in my ears. What if they raped my sister and my friend? What if they killed them?

"Leave us alone," I shouted.

Lois said she was hungry. The boys said they could fix that. She was sleepy. They could fix that, too. Lois stood up. Jane, too.

"If you get in that car, I'll never speak to you again." I was afraid I'd never see them again!

"I'm not getting in that car," I declared. "I'm staying right here."

The boys encouraged Lois and Jane not to pay attention to the "bossy one," the "scaredy cat." The thought of leaving without me evidently persuaded Lois to stay. She sat back down on the concrete bench. The boys drove on.

In a few minutes, however, the green Studebaker turned back into the cemetery. I was really scared then. We were going to be kidnapped! As from a script, we all repeated our lines, but that time with my additional threat that I'd call the police. They peeled out of the cemetery.

We took up our suitcases and walked out on Main Street. But the cohesion we'd had setting out on The Great Escape had been broken. I sensed a coup in the making. It was Lois who pushed me aside and hailed a policeman driving slowly down the street. If he was looking for criminals, maybe we'd suffice.

"We ran away from school," Lois told him.

The officer wanted to know what school, when, who, phone number of the nearest of kin. He called the Station and said he was bringing in "three run-away girls".

When we arrived at the police station, Aunt Rachel was already there talking with the police matron who looked very spiffy in her uniform. The matron asked why we'd run away and, as we told her, Aunt Rachel seemed subdued—as if she were hearing our complaints for the first time. She did not scold us on the way back to Chickasha. She took Bud to a doctor.

The next month, Daddy and Aunt Rachel helped Bud move into a boys' boarding school in Subiaco, Arkansas. Bud loved it. He spent summers with Daddy.

That was the last Year of Innocence. The dark shadow of Hitler's swastika lay over most of Europe. Americans, Sister Lily told me, were rightly enraged, but Roosevelt was too cautious. Then came Pearl Harbor. Sister Lily seemed relieved; finally America was in the War.

Suddenly soldiers and sailors were on every sidewalk. Girls sprang up, too—in tight sweaters walking arm in arm with their guy; sometimes proudly pregnant. War seemed to have excited Eros. Love was in the air and I, in the tenth grade, inhaled deeply.

I fell in love.

It was my first "in love" experience and, like all first loves, unbelievably intense. His name was Padraic. He was a day student, two years ahead of me, full of Irish charm. But boarder-day student romances faced logistic hurdles for boarders. Where and when and how to meet? For Padraic and me the upper porch became the favored site. Dinner hour seemed the safest time. Being a laundry-worker proved helpful. I found it simple to leave the refectory under pretext of needing to finish folding towels. From the laundry room, I dashed to the porch where my love was waiting for me. I never got caught.

Padraic liked to talk. He talked about engineering programs at Oklahoma University. I listened, but always I was waiting for him to embrace me. I couldn't get enough touch. I remember peeling out of my coat even on cold days so I could feel more of him. Later I would learn my need had a name: skin hunger.

I mooned and primped and drew hearts and flowers around Padraic's initials; his last name began with C—a bowl-shaped letter that I filled with paper kisses. But Padraic and I couldn't go to the movies or out to dinner or take a walk in the park; we were limited to meeting on the upper porch while the nuns were at table. Every boarders' romance stumbled over these constraining logistics. The romance between Padraic and me lasted almost a year. It ended when two boarders whose own romances had floundered told me that Padraic had told them he didn't like me anymore. Maybe he had said that. Maybe not. Whatever the facts, the romance ended with the usual heartbreak. At least for me. Padraic seemed mystified. One day when he extended his dear, Irish arm out to detain me after Latin class, I brushed by him haughtily, my heart aching.

Padraic, you will never know how I had planned that Latin-class meeting and rehearsed that haughty walk.

That was the year we begged Aunt Rachel to put us in a different boarding school. "There's one in Guthrie. Jane's going there." Jane's folks seemed willing to put her any place. Just not home.

"Well," Aunt Rachel said, "I'll talk to your father." We knew, then, that we'd go to Guthrie.

If the leghorns hadn't escaped their pen the day Aunt Rachel drove Lois and me to the so-called campus of St. Joseph's, I might not have so immediately loved the place. A vineyard marched up and over a gentle hill northeast of the main building and a potato patch lay between it and a garden. A lean dog, part greyhound, yawned, stretched and lumbered down the front steps of an old brick building to smell the car tires. A nun wearing a peasant-like habit was lugging a large watermelon from the far garden. And there were those three escaped hens pecking in the rose bed. I thought of pictures I'd seen in the encyclopedia in the cloak room in Chickasha. Had we driven into the 16th century?

The sense of history was almost palpable. In 1889, three Benedictine nuns—Mother Paula O'Reilly, and Sisters Anselma Kelly and Angela

McMammey—arrived in Guthrie, the capitol of Oklahoma Territory. Guthrie was still a city of tents, but that's where Mother Paula wanted to spend her substantial inheritance to build a convent with room for a boarding school. She would name the building "St. Joseph's."

After hiring an attorney to argue with her brother who had become hostile to all things Catholic, Mother Paula O'Reilly finally wrested enough inheritance money to build the squat brick building to which we arrived that August, 1944. Besides being part day school, part boarding school, and part Motherhouse, St. Joseph's was also home to a few surviving centipedes and tarantulas whose ancestors had been displaced when builders dug into the red soil of a small hill a few miles west of Guthrie. Fifty-four years later, I would call that old building home.

"Oh, you made it." Jane, already there and unpacked, came bounding out the front door and embraced Lois and me warmly as if we'd been apart two years instead of two months. "What do you think? So far?" She wanted us to like the place she'd recommended. We did.

The move from Chickasha to Guthrie was a kind of culture shock. For one thing, it was a real farm: milk cows, chicken pens, wheat fields, a cow pond in a pasture, and gardens. We walked on dirt paths instead of on concrete sidewalks. Fences were unnecessary. We heard different sounds —Gregorian chant, the lowing of cattle, roosters; we smelled different odors—rose petal pulp for Mother Agnes' rosary industry, manure, old books, alfalfa. Almost daily, the aroma of baking bread drifted upstairs from the bakery.

Sister Benedict Marie, a rosy-cheeked farm girl from Kansas, our prefect, led us to the dormitory. In Chickasha, we'd grown used to tiny alcoves, narrow beds and iron bedsteads. Nothing new there. But despite the crowdedness, the dorm in Guthrie seemed airy. Almost cool, in fact. The ceilings were high. Uncurtained windows stretched from near the floor almost to the ceiling. Each window sill was wide enough to sit on. To sit hugging your knees and gazing over the landscape like Ann of Green Gables.

Thirty years later, Job Corps students would call the 54-year-old building *Big Red Ugly* and eventually raze it. But in 1945, I loved every inch of it, creaking floors, hissing radiators, leaking faucets—all of it. To me, the weathered barn was a south-leaning poem.

Mornings, I awoke to the sound of nuns chanting Lauds. Gregorian chant became a familiar sound, a lovely lonely sound. For some reason— maybe it was the plaintiveness—the sound aroused in me a sense of loss, and with that, memories of my mother. She began to enter my dreams— seldom in ways or places I'd expect.

> In a dream, I flew. I unlatched the door
> of sleep and, weightless as fog, lifted
> above the dark houses and drifted, slow.
>
> Below me Lake Placid carried on its
> back a load of stars, winking at their
> unreachable sisters hanging silent
>
> from the blue-black ceiling. I saw
> my mother (luminous, now) dancing
> in an elm tree's green arms and singing
>
> in a language people learn after death.
> (My dream-self understood
> the words.) There are many ways to fly.

I thought often of my mother. Daddy had kept her scrapbook and brought it to the house at Sacred Heart. He had placed it on a table in the parlor. Since we rarely entered that room, going in to turn the pages of her scrapbook had always seemed a formal, almost a reverent, affair. Sometimes I'd go alone into the parlor, page through her scrapbook and try to imagine her there in far-away Michigan. There was one snapshot of her at the oil camp we called Blue Heaven. She was standing beside the sweet peas she'd planted.

Then the house had burned and everything in it. The memory of my mother was fading and I began trying to find her in the faces of the mothering nuns.

Of course, not all the nuns could be described as mothering. As a matter of fact, many of those dusty-shoed women were "characters" worthy of a James Thurber sketch.

"Why does Sister Constance sit in the hallway during Benediction?" I asked Pat Kruger. Pat—"The Almanac," the girls called her—had been at St. Joseph's two years. Sister Albert Marie was Pat's mother's sister, so Pat had an inside source

"She's allergic to incense."

"She wears white stockings, too."

"That's because black dye makes her ankles break out into a rash," Pat said. Then like a spy divulging secrets, "That's one story. Some of the nuns think she just wants to be different."

Other facts I learned from Pat:

* Sister Martina was a Cherokee princess; her father was a chief.

* Sister Augusta entered the convent when she was 14 years old and still didn't know how babies were made.

* Sister Petronilla's dad had been shot in a street in Mexico for harboring a priest. He was a martyr. Neighbors dipped handkerchiefs in his blood.

* Sister Regina, born in Scotland, could yodel before she could talk.

* And this juicy one: Sister Gabrielle had once been married. One night, mistaking her husband for a burglar, she'd shot him dead. She had to get a special dispensation to join the community. "She's a little crazy, you know. But harmless."

But it wasn't the zany nuns with their assorted foibles that shocked me. It was the classes. They turned my neatly-arranged scholastic world upside-down.

Enter: Sister Mary Alice who taught Theology.

Liturgical Renewal?

Dorothy Day?

Soup Kitchens?

Peter Maurin and his "Little Essays" in *The Catholic Worker*?

Social Justice?

It all belonged to a world unknown to me and even, I guessed, unknown to Sister Amadeus in Chickasha. None of the new information had been available in the blue catechism I used to memorize or, for that matter, in any book I'd read sitting on the cloakroom floors in the sixth grade, seventh, eighth, even the ninth and tenth grades?

It took a while to absorb the fact that this, too, was Catholicism. I found it less cerebral and more compassionate.

Enter: Sister Mary Andrew and Literature class.

e. e. cummings?

Issa's haikus?

Pearl Buck's *The Good Earth*?

"Eddie Mae, on Monday, please prepare to explain to the class how Lotus and O-lan typify the condition of women in China in the 19th century."

Sometimes after Sister Mary Andrew's class I'd walk to the grotto with one of Issa's haikus, trying to reconcile the unrhymed, unmetered words with what I knew of poetry. After Monsignor Monaghan's visit to our class in Chickasha, I'd grown to love Francis Thompson's poetry. I still do. But this? Nevertheless, I remember reciting aloud,

"In this world we walk / on the roof of hell / gazing at flowers," and being conscious in a new way of the hot roiling core of the earth beneath my feet and the miracle of things growing at my feet. The dusty old cedars that lined the path and the limp pink zinnias at the base of the grotto caused in me a rush of amazement.

Then there was e. e. cummings—the guy that clearly had never diagrammed a sentence. What's more, Sister Mary Andrew never once mentioned the lack of punctuation. "Notice," she said instead, "the balance of the two five-line stanzas and the slant rhyme of place and peace." Slant, indeed. She handed us a mimeographed poem: "love is a place / & through this place of / love moves / (with brightness of peace) / all places." Love is a place?

Sister Mary Andrew and Sister Mary Alice were clearly cut of the same cloth, both of them emphasizing compassion.

Enter: Sister Mary Placida. Art teacher.

Sister Mary Placida was deformed.

"She was born that way," Pat told me. "They almost didn't let her in."

"Why? Because she has a hump on her back?"

"Yeah, at first they were afraid she couldn't handle the schedule and the work load. But I guess they finally figured that if she could get a Master's Degree in Art at Oklahoma University, she could handle a monastery. I heard that, when she was born, the doctor said she'd die before her first birthday."

As a matter of fact, Sister Mary Placida lived 20 more years and became one of my dearest friends in the convent. When Advent season appeared on the liturgical calendar, Sister Mary Alice enlisted Sister Mary Placida to teach us to create Christmas cards. The same for Easter. First, we tried not to cut ourselves as we carved linoleum blocks and then not to cut the silk as we peeled away wax for serigraphs. Pat made beautiful work. My cards were more third-grader quality. I chose the least smeared to send Aunt Rachel. She must have been mystified. I felt stupid. "You may not have the skill, but you have the soul of an artist," Sister Mary Placida said. I suppose she meant to console.

Willard Stone, the great part-Cherokee sculptor, used to travel to the monastery to visit Sister Mary Placida in the art studio. There they talked symbolism, wood grain, color, Cherokee history. They talked birds, rural Oklahoma, poverty. They talked God, spirituality, the aloneness of artists. I know because, while I double-cleaned brushes, I eavesdropped. Listening to them I glimpsed for the first time a connection between art and spirituality.

When Thomas Gilcrease offered Willard the position of artist-in-residence at Gilcrease Museum in Tulsa. Sister Mary Placida was relieved. "The Stones have ten children, you know," she told me." They need the stipend."

Enter: Sister Regina, habit hiked almost to her Scottish knees, strong legs pumping the old organ, teaching us to read notes that were on square clefs that had four lines. Forget keys. Forget measures. Throw the metronome out the window. "No, no, girls. Chant simply flows. It's a river, and like a river, it doesn't stop." She also taught Glee Club but always made sure we knew that modern music followed Gregorian by five centuries. "Think of it, girls. Five hundred years! There wouldn't be any Beethoven if there hadn't first been Gregorian notation."

Toward the end of that year, the seniors and even some of the juniors began to talk about what they'd do after graduation. To them, the world was full of promise. To me, it was full of danger. Concentration camps. Dead soldiers. Gold stars in windows. Wanda killing the cat. My mother dying. My absent father. Greasy-haired boys trying to entice three runaway girls into a car.

On the second-floor stair landing, I sat on one of the wide window sills and gazed out at as much of the world as I could see from there. In the distance, someone was driving a toy-sized combine across a postage-stamp wheat field. A half-inch truck drove soundlessly onto the field. A speck of driver emerged and the field swallowed him. The way history swallows people and events. The way the world would swallow me.

Why did I suddenly remember Sister Mary Lawrence's biology class and her remark about the mayflies thick above the cow pond: "They hatch, mature, mate, lay eggs, and die in one place. To them, the cow pond is the world." Safe. Contained.

Sister Mary Alice had assured us that from the little chapel in Guthrie, the spiritual energy of prayer radiates. It's unseen, she'd said, but powerful. I imagined a worker dead tired and cranky being unknowingly touched by prayer-energy and being surprised by an impulse to smile. Maybe I could be a sender of spiritual energy.

I went downstairs and knocked on Mother Rita's office door. "I want to enter the convent."

In Oklahoma City, Aunt Rachel went with me downtown to Brown's Department Store to buy black lisle stockings and black shoes. "Not too clunky," I said.

Back at Guthrie, Sister Margarita, the novice mistress, handed me a black mid-calf dress and short cape to complete my outfit. She explained the ritual for asking permission to join the Sisters. "The Sisters," she said, "will be in Chapter."
Chapter?

I hastened to Pat, The Almanac. "What's Chapter?"

Pat explained that "Chapter" referred to a decision-making meeting of all the Sisters who've made Final Profession of Vows. "The Sisters' dining room is also their Chapter Room."

I entered the Sisters' dining/chapter room. The nuns had pushed their chairs away from table as a way to signify this was not mealtime. The tables formed an inverted U with an open sea of floor between dark shores. The mainland lay far in front. I bowed to the right shore, to the left shore, to the mainland. Then I knelt on the concrete ocean and unfolded the shaking paper on which I'd written my lines. "For Jesus' sake," I read, "may I be permitted to join your Community in the Benedictine way of life?" On the mainland, Mother Rosalene nodded slightly and smiled slightly. I stood and followed Sister Margarita into the next 20 years of my life.

I had just turned 17. It was 1945.

Lois, barely 15, entered the Community a few months later. So did Jane, 16. Lois and I had to stick together. Jane was like our sister. I don't know whether accepting candidates so young was a typical practice of other Benedictine Communities at that time or whether it was just the practice of the Benedictines in Guthrie. Since Canon Law stipulated that a woman couldn't take final vows before she was 20, entering the convent at a young age meant a long novitiate. Lois was in the novitiate a long time.

After a six-month candidacy, the professed Sisters met in Chapter and voted to accept some of the candidates into the canonical novitiate. In 1945, Chapter votes were still cast by dropping beans into a jar: white beans for acceptance, red beans for rejection. I suppose this custom was left over from the Middle Ages when most women were illiterate.

Sister Margarita explained the rules to us: "The canonical year is meant to be a contemplative period during which you can immerse yourself in Benedictine spirituality. It's a quiet time that may not be broken by distraction. Therefore there will be no visits to or from your family. No letters to or from your family."

"How about friends who aren't related to you?" Jane always pushed.

"It stands to reason, doesn't it, Miss Jane, that if you aren't allowed to visit with your parents, you wouldn't be allowed to communicate with a school chum or a next-door neighbor." Sister Margarita bent her mouth in irritation. Jane was proud of her ability to rankle the novice mistress.

"What if you need to go to a doctor, or what if your grandma dies?"

Sister Margarita sighed darkly. Jane didn't care. By barely a bean or two, the nuns had voted to let her receive the habit. By Golly, she was in.

Five of us—Jane, me, and three other candidates prepared for the ceremony. It was a big deal. Guests were invited. The bishop would pontificate. We novices-to-be would enter the chapel in wedding gowns to signify becoming brides of Christ. At a given point in the ceremony, we would exit the chapel to don the full habit with one difference: novices wore white veils instead of black ones. After re-entering the chapel and lying prostrate under a funeral pall to symbolize that we had become dead to the world, the bishop would give each of us our Sister-name. New person, new name.

Jane wanted to know if the ceremony was described in the Benedictine Rule. It wasn't. Nevertheless we were excited about the upcoming ritual. After all, the wedding gown part of the service would be our last appearance as lay persons and we wanted to be beautiful.

The five of us climbed to the attic—called Seventh Heaven—and opened the closet wherein hung six wedding gowns that had been donated by pious former brides. Since the gown's fabric was typically fragile and possibly old, we couldn't take them in or let them out or hem them up. The other candidates found gowns close to their size, I had to settle for an ivory gown several sizes too big and several inches too long with a bust line several cup sizes too generous. Besides that, ivory was not my color; it made my skin look sallow. How could I make my last appearance even passably attractive? My only hope lay in my hair. It was thick and held curl. Rollers were out of the question so, after my shampoo the night before the ceremony, I ventured into the boarders' dorm and scavenged some bobby pins so I could pin my hair into waves. The problem: no hair dryer. The morning of the ceremony, my hair fell damp and straight.

I don't know why I fretted about my less-than-beautiful last appearance. I couldn't invite my father because I had no address. Aunt Rachel came but the entire ceremony left her completely baffled. Afterward, she said "Congratulations" but couldn't figure out how to kiss me without dislodging the headdress. Jane had no guests.

Before the ceremony, each of us had written three names we'd like to have. Since we didn't know whether the abbess would choose one of our suggestions or not, we waited anxiously to hear the bishop announce the name we were to be called the rest of our lives My first choice had been Judith. I don't know what Jane had written, but Columba was not one of them.

"Henceforth, you will be known as Sister Judith," the bishop said to me. Jane's new name was Sister Columba.

The first order of business was mastering the art of wearing the habit. When ascending stairs, I learned to lift daintily the front of the long skirt; when descending I kept it from dragging by gathering yardage to the side. When bending over (as we often did in the garden) I learned to lift the habit's front hem and pin it behind. Keeping our eyes cast modestly down, as Sister Margarita had advised, was easy. One never knew when one's habit might sweep up a centipede. There weren't really that many of the orange-and-black crawlers, but it didn't take many to inspire wariness.

For most of us, making coifs (called wimples in most other Orders) was the great stumbling block. The twice-starched linen was dampened, spread out on a board (not unlike a bread board), and pleated into tiny pleats. My coifs tended to be a bit cockeyed. Sometimes I conned Sister Edith into pleating mine.

Despite my difficulties making coifs and the childish games we played during recreation (like Drop the Hankerchief), for me the Novitiate Year was a halcyon season. I loved farm life. We gathered and spun honey. We picked pecans. At midnight on Christmas we walked to the barn and sang "Away in a Manger" in a cow stall. We planted gardens, harvested fruit, dug potatoes. We milked cows. I was usually assigned milk duty with Sister Edith because she was experienced. In order to finish milking in time for Lauds, we got up at 4:30 and donned what we called milk habits.

> They hung on nails near battered buckets
> on the screened porch beside the kitchen.
> Made of cotton and washed so many Mondays
> in Sister Loretta's lye soap,
> they'd faded to various hues—
>
> blue-black, greenish, charcoal gray.
> Yesterday's milkers had left streaks of salt
> under the arms and along the yokes.
> They were short (relatively speaking)
> having been frayed,
> cut off time and again and re-hemmed.
> When it was my morning to milk, I'd choose
> one and skip to the barn feeling girlish
> wearing almost a dress, almost a color,
> a light swish flirting mid-calf.

During the Novitiate Year, I also became skilled in using the breviary and pronouncing Latin. I learned to juggle the heavy *Liber Usualis*, the book that held all he chants for various feast days. On feast days, our chant flowed like a river washing, I imagined, over the world, over especially all the oil-field camps in Oklahoma. On ordinary days, we chanted on one tone, *G*. When Sister Regina played the organ, she kept us on key by improvising music that included plenty of G chords. But when we chanted without an organist, we tended to flatten. Not a true flat, but a crack somewhere between *G* and *G*-flat. Mother Rita, cursed with perfect pitch, found the sound maddening. When she could bear it no longer, she stomped to the organ and repeatedly plunked *G G G*.

Although I loved Gregorian chant, I dreaded chapel. We were crowded eight to a pew built for six. Especially in hot weather the mixed odors of female bodies, black dye, and sweaty habits hung blanket-like. The smell was especially offensive on days we cleaned chickens. When the chapel bell rang on those days, we simply wiped our hands free of wet feathers, rolled our sleeves down, and went to Vespers.

Cleaning chickens was the most dreaded job. Sister Humiliata always cried. With her hands occupied, she lifted her arm and wiped her nose on her sleeve But she dried her tears long enough to complain about having to wear her habit during the job. "Who made that rule?"

Waking up was difficult for me. Each morning Sister Margarita came into the dorm and said cheerily, "Benedicite" to which the novices (minus me) responded, "Deo Gratias." In 20 minutes, we were supposed to jump up, make our beds, wash our faces, dress, and enter the chapel. I was late almost every morning. St. Benedict insisted in his Rule that any interference in the Divine Office merited "making satisfaction."

Leaving the rest of the Community to begin prayer without my help was such an offense and required making satisfaction, or *culpa*, a kind of wordless apology. In chapel, *culpa* was made with a series of yoga-like postures: 1.) genuflecting in the middle aisle, 2.) bowing to the Sisters on the right side and then to those on the left, 3.) kneeling in the middle aisle, 4.) touching one's fingers to the floor, 5.) then kissing one's fingers. "In earlier days," Sister Mary Margarita explained, "monks used to prostrate and kiss the floor." I was satisfied with kissing fingers that had touched the floor. In just a few short months, I honed chapel *culpa* to an art.

A single oscillating fan tried to stir the thick chapel air. The fan's sound—*chuff, chuff, chuff, chuff*—often took me back to Blue Heaven where the steady drum of oil pumps had once lulled me to sleep.

> In the chapel in the sticky summer
> morning, the whir   click   whir
> of the oscillating fan
> winnows silence like chaff.
>
> I watch Sister Sylvester's precisely pressed
> veil lift in light welcome
> to the fan's brief pass of air.
>
> In a pew in front of me, Sister Walburga
> finally accepts the fan's droning
> invitation and lets her head slump
> steeply floorward.
>
> Beyond the open windows, the sun
> rises with fierce vigor.
> And the chapel fan moves
> forth   and   back.
> Half a mile away, truckers shift to second gear
> on the steamy hill. Sound carries me
>
> back to Blue Heaven—
> the *chuff-chuff* of pumping units
> rising   falling.

With Sister Margarita as novice mistress, daily Novitiate Instructions included not just the Holy Rule of St. Benedict but also poetry and art. In the afternoons Sister Mary Placida taught us calligraphy. We read the French poet, Charles Pequy. Sometimes during what we called recreation, we darned stockings while Sister Margarita read to us passages from G. K.Chesterton or Carol Houselander. We discussed Leon Bloy's *Pilgrim of the Absolute* and *Vipers' Tangle by Mauriac.*

I loved the balance of art and labor. We moved from milking the cows to singing Gregorian chant, from spinning honey to reading poetry. To me, every day was a medieval poem. One of the most memorable days involved digging potatoes.

> A green sky blots the lowering sun.
> In the distance, a grumble of thunder.
> This morning, Mr. Porter turned
> the soil and now potatoes lie loose
> and half-exposed. *We must bring them in*
> *before the storm*, says the abbess. *We'll pray*
> *Compline while we work*. Two dozen
> of us in voluminous habits gather
> hems waist high and pin them behind us
> like untidy bustles. Fingering for tubers
> we wait for Sister Mary Joan to intone:
> *Deus in adjutorium, meum intende.*
> Our voices bobble across the field carrying
> their loads of psalms. Darkness has rendered
> us invisible. In what we call *Grand Silence*,
> little rags of sound mix in the dark—
> dry swish of habits
> dull thump of potatoes dropped into galvanized buckets.
> The whole world is hushed.

The Community in Guthrie was extraordinarily poor. Sister Sheila's brother had installed the water-pump, a rebuilt bargain. The pump was faulty; water to the third floor was sporadic, and the fourth-floor stool sat in its nook like an empty promise. But the labor of putting in the water pump had been donated, so who could complain. Sister Martin skimmed the milk and sold most of the cream in Guthrie. The tin pitchers we used at table showed their age in dents. Each breviary had been used by someone sleeping in the cemetery. The pages were brown and brittle. Bed sheets, table cloths, and habits held up under patches. But we didn't care. We were young. Being poor was part of the great adventure.

"We don't need a vow of poverty," Jane explained to our unsmiling novice mistress when the water pump broke again. "We've got the real McCoy."

Just as labor balanced learning, so poverty balanced a kind of country elegance. Take the dining room for instance. When we ran out of enough glassware, we set the table with jelly glasses, courtesy of the Aaron Jelly Company. The flatware didn't match. Cracks zigzagged across plates. But we ate on white tablecloths and placed table-knives one inch from the edge of the table and the jelly glass one inch above the tip of the knife. On feast days, we graced each table with a bouquet. Zinnias in summer or colored leaves in autumn. Poor but elegant.

To me, labor never felt like drudgery. Poverty never felt ugly.

Unlike some medieval horror stories about self-flogging or other such practices, Benedictines went easy on self punishment. The closest we came was in the Chapter of Faults. About once a month, the nuns met in the Dining/Chapter Room, and any Sister who had done something that disturbed the order of the monastery (breaking a dish, coming late to chapel, talking during Nocturnal Silence) asked pardon in a simple ritual. Kneeling in the middle of the cement space between the rows of nuns, we said, "For Jesus' sake, I beg pardon for _____."

Jane thought Chapter of Faults was ridiculous. "What does Jesus have to do with breaking a dish? Nothing. If you ask me, the whole thing's just plain silly." She made her point by accusing herself of "sliding down the banister when the bishop was here" or "making Elaine, the cow, sick by not stripping the last of her milk". The novices and some of the professed Sister would snicker and Sister Margarita would frown.

To me, the year of novitiate was a blissful dream.

When I heard we were planning to build a hospital in nearby Guthrie, I was astonished. You mean there's a 20th-century town right at our feet? Just three miles west? And we can go there from here, across centuries? For it still seemed to me that the monastery existed in a kind of invisible space and time. "We need to engage the community more," Sister Margarita said. "We need to be a service in Guthrie."

Besides being home to the largest Masonic Temple in America, Guthrie was a historic place in its own right.

In the space of a few hours, the town of Guthrie had sprung up from prairie to become the largest city west of the Mississippi River. The "Queen of the Prairie," as the little town was called, quickly became the capital of Oklahoma Territory. What had begun as a tent-city had turned into a town befitting its position as capital—brick buildings, municipal water and electricity, laws prohibiting spitting on the sidewalks so ladies with long skirts could arrive at their destinations with dry hems. Wealthy people built homes with railed porches, pitched roofs, balconies, double-hung windows. Guthrie fairly sparkled. Oklahoma Territory became the State of Oklahoma in 1907. Guthrie was its capitol for three years. Then came stories of the robbery that changed the course of state history. The story goes this way: under cover of darkness; someone stole the capital seal and carried it to Oklahoma City. Guthrie reeled from the blow and seemed ready to die. The little town did not die; but it slipped, in a manner of speaking, into a coma.

About the time the Benedictines were thinking "hospital," Guthrie was waking up and thinking "image makeover." Whereas Oklahoma City had razed many old downtown buildings, Guthrie had maintained much of its late 19th-century architecture. Tourists and students of architecture traveled to Guthrie–which, today, has reinvented itself as a bona fide Historic District.

Years before Guthrie began to wake up, someone had begun building a hospital and, unable to complete the job, had left the windowless corpse on the north side of Guthrie. Our little community proposed to finish the job. Sister Ursula oversaw the structure's completion and supervised the business of making the building into a much-needed medical facility.

Benedictine Heights Hospital opened in 1948. Lois, who would have the name Sister Mary Carol, would work there.

At the end of the canonical year, Jane was voted out of the Community. In those days, departing nuns left during the night and communication with them was cut off. I didn't know Jane was gone until the next morning at breakfast. I never saw her again. Not only had I lost a near-sister but all of us novices had lost the excitement and sane commentary Jane had provided. We knew Sister Margarita had given a negative report about Jane and we felt resentful, but we lacked the nerve to express our feelings.

We wanted to get the black veil, the sign that we'd pronounced temporary vows.

Several years later, a rodeo came to town and Lois, who was working then at the hospital in Guthrie, received a phone call. It was Jane. She had married a rodeo rider. "He calls me Calamity Jane," she'd bragged. "We have a daughter named Judith Carol–for you guys."

In the ceremony for making temporary (three-year) vows, I made five promises: to be obedient, to practice poverty, to be chaste, to strive for perfection (conversion of morals), and to remain at St. Joseph 's Monastery (stability). The ceremony was meant to set us on a three-year study period called *scholasticate*. Our scholastic mistress was Sister Mary Geraldine, an easy-going woman uninterested in study. So I began to haunt the library. But, with Jane gone, I had no one to share ideas with. That's when I realized that a major part of the pleasure of reading lay in talking over ideas.

The monastery's magic began to diminish. Where was learning? Poetry?

Aunt Rachel's family had moved to Arizona because Uncle Fergus's cough had worsened. Bud was at Subiaco. Jane seemed to have dropped off the edge of the world. Lois was still in the Novitiate and the stricter rules prohibited our talking together. Too many changes for a girl who'd become a nun as much to secure a haven as to serve the world by teaching America's young. I missed the inspiration and heady excitement I'd known as a student and a novice. Newcomers to the novitiate seemed to arrive with catechism mentalities. The novitiate year began to fade like a dream. Like a scene in a waterglobe after the shook snow has fallen. Life in rhythm with the natural world, time for learning and contemplation—that life was myth. It must have been the vision Mother Paula had when she used much of her inherited money to build a Motherhouse in Indian Territory. But reality and vision have always been at war. And the reality was poverty. There was work to do. Money to be made. Boarders. Hospitals. Schools. It was time to grow up and I found it bitter.

Martha, a new candidate, was walking head down on the path circling the Marian statue. She was homesick. I remembered homesickness, the hollowed out feeling.

I walked with her.

-Do you feel like your body is empty? –Yes.

-I want to go home.

–Go, then. You should go.

But she didn't go. It may have been books that held Martha there. Books and someone to share them with. Even on days of silence—which most days were—Martha and I met in the library, excited over one of Peter

Maurin's woodcuts in the Catholic Worker or about a poem or new novel. We whispered. We giggled over sex passages in novels. Sometimes Sister Mary Rose, the librarian, scolded us. But since she, too, loved books, we figured that she wouldn't report us for breaking silence. Martha discovered a few of Daniel Berrigan's early poems. We read G. K.Chesterton. G. B. Shaw. We waded through Maritain's *The Person and the Common Good* and Abbot Marmion's *Commentary on the Rule of St. Benedict.*

We read novels, too. Graham Greene. Bernanos. Sigrid Undset. I especially liked Undset because her stories, set in the Middle Ages, reminded me of the monastery I had experienced as a boarder and, later, as a novice. I loved living in the 16th century.

On the rare days that didn't hold time enough to hold all the words we wanted to say, Martha suggested that darkness be a good time for spillover.

I found it easy to observe the Rule of Silence. I loved the hush that fell in the convent and over the country, especially at night when the world seemed to go to sleep. So when Martha suggested that we complete our conversations during Nocturnal Silence, I felt a bit reluctant.

"Are we bothering anyone? Are we keeping anyone awake? Didn't Benedict stress Nocturnal Silence as a courtesy to the others?" I hated it when Martha argued with questions.

So after Compline and lights out in the dorm, we tiptoed sometimes outside in our nightgowns. The unused side entrance provided the ideal spot. With a brick, Martha propped the door to prevent our getting locked out.

Night is a kind of darkroom in which sounds became sharp. Locusts. Tree frogs. Occasional traffic on the highway which lay about 150 feet in front of us. Rustling leaves. Silence, even. It was like an auditory picture brought sharply into focus.

One night the sound made when a trucker shifted gears on the dark highway carried me back to Blue Heaven. "My dad used to drive a truck," I said. Martha said nothing. Often when we talked about the past, we spoke less to one another than to the night. It was a little like dreaming out loud. That particular night, I told the darkness how we had lived in the oil-field camp with my mother; how, when we heard Daddy's truck, Mother would freshen her lipstick and the three of us would run out to hug our greasy Daddy; how he'd wash his hands in the kitchen with gritty gray soap and throw the water out the back door in a silver arc; how he'd comb his hair and put on clean khakis and draw our mother to his lap.

I fell into a kind of trance. I shifted into present tense. "His forehead is real white here where his hat keeps the sun out."

Martha was silent for several minutes. Then, softly, "That little girl lives in you still."

Like Russian nesting dolls, I thought. Lift the nun doll and beneath it, there's a girl doll in a boarding school. Under that one, there's the small camp-kid doll. All my selves. Still breathing. I felt relieved. My garb and new name hadn't snuffed out their lives, after all.

Father Carpentier, a Frenchman from a wealthy family, was the monastery chaplain. He had joined a Dominican Order, and always wore the Dominican habit. He also wore, almost constantly, a biretta (the three-cornered hat worn by many Catholic clergy).

Despite his wealthy background—or perhaps because of it—Father Carpentier's practice of poverty was extreme. So extreme, it became fabled among Oklahoma Catholics. He never had money. He never owned a car. He seemed not to believe in ownership, his or anyone else's. Once while helping out at a well-furnished rectory, a homeless man came to the door and walked away with the absent pastor's favorite chair and a rare painting. "You can sell them at the flea market on 9th Street," Father Carpentier would say. The wily gift-giver's only observable pride lay in the military medals he earned in World War I. He carried them always and was happy to talk about the years he'd served as chaplain in the famed Rainbow Division where he'd earned both the Croix de Guerre and the Distinguished Service Cross.

Father Carpentier had walked into Guthrie in 1946 with the intention of establishing a ministry to the blacks; but in typical Catholic church fashion, he had to do double duty by also being monastery chaplain. His heart wasn't in it. He'd much rather ramble into Sister Petronilla's kitchen, wrap a hunk of bread or an apple in newspaper, tuck it under his biretta and set out on the 10- or 12-mile walk to Langston—a town settled by African Americans when they had hoped to make Oklahoma a black state. Besides using his biretta for a lunch pail, Father Carpentier used his hip pocket for a tabernacle in which he carried some consecrated hosts. "Do you love Jesus?" he would ask a black child. "Yes, Father." And the man from France would reach into his hip pocket, whip out the gold pyx, and give the child Holy Communion on the spot.

He was not a stickler for rules or labels. Once, in the confessional, when I confessed having doubts about my vocation, he loudly proclaimed "Doubt? That's not a sin!" I was tempted to explain to him that it was hard to commit a really good sin in the monastery environs.

During that year, I taught Grades 4-5-6. I was 20 years old. Children came from town to attend monastery classes. The school was unaccredited by the state but probably quite excellent because it was where we first practiced the teaching art, and we desperately wanted to do a bang-up job. I loved teaching. I remembered how, at St. Joseph's in Chickasha, three grades in a room offered chances for both review and advanced learning. I learned to teach long division to the fifth graders while keeping an eye on the fourth and sixth graders.

Besides teaching and completing high school, I was assigned that year to prefect (take care of) the boys. Boys from 6 to 12 years old could board at the monastery. The boys' dorm was in what we called "The Lodge" down by Lake Placid, a mosquito-infested cow pond with water the color of tomato soup. The long path from The Lodge to the Motherhouse lay past the cemetery, the orchard, and a pasture pretty much owned by a bull with an enormous ring in its nose and enormous testicles swinging between his hind legs. The path between The Lodge and the Motherhouse was lined with bridal-wreath bushes. Besides teaching and prefecting, I studied history and college math. My schedule left precious little opportunity for monastic life. Walking toward the Motherhouse, I'd sometimes hear the Sisters chanting. Was I really a member of the Community? Was too-much-to-do and too-little-time-to-do-it-in what the future held? It did not occur to me that I was unhappy.

> I wasn't a bride
> nor hoped
> to be those days.
>
> My hose and habit,
> black as hunger,
> resisted the bridal

wreath blooming
along the path
to The Lodge

where parents
boarded their young
sons, leaving me

to teach them
to write cursive
and kneel at night

to pray,
lay me down.
What I remember

is how petals
delicate as lace
lay slender

limbs at my feet
and spilled seed pearls
on dry ground.

Nowella, a girl working her way through the monastery's small college, was assigned to watch over the boys after school, thus giving me a chance to join the Sisters for Vespers. Sometimes she showed up.

Even though I often felt overwhelmed, the year held joy. I liked spending time with the boy boarders. I liked the students in my classroom. But Nowella was a pain. And I missed monastic life.

It was a honey-and-vinegar period.

At the end of May, the boys went home for the summer. I locked up The Lodge and moved back into the Motherhouse. The Sisters who had been teaching at various schools returned home. (We called the Motherhouse: *home*.)

In the summers we usually spent recreation—the time between supper and Compline—outdoors. By threes or fours, some nuns would stroll to the grotto; a few would get up a game of baseball; most of us sat on folding chairs in a big circle and talked or sang folk songs. We sang a lot. I imagined our voices drifting over the landscape like a flock of starlings rising fluid as a scarf. After the Compline bells rang, some nuns were apt to go humming to chapel. Mother Maurita frowned them to silence.

Our voices were strong but untrained, a problem remedied by Mr. Skaupsi.

When Congress passed the "Displaced Persons Act of 1948," the Guthrie Benedictines sponsored Mr. and Mrs. Skaupski, both of whom had fought in the Polish Underground. Before Hitler sent unwelcome troops into Poland and Gorgy Skaupski joined the Resistance, he had been a concert pianist and a choral director. After arriving in Guthrie, he set about teaching his new Benedictine family how to sing polyphony. The classes were held in St. Cecilia's Music Hall, a thinly insulated frame building squatting beyond the trees Mother Paula O'Reilly had planted before statehood. Weather may have been one of the biggest adjustments for the Skaupis. Inside the music hall, the temperature soared and Mr. Skaupski sweated enormously, but he popped salt pills and both disciplined and inspired us.

"When the bell is ringink, we are singink," he scolded when we straggled in. So we hiked up our skirts and scurried to be on time for class with the man who never got the hang of "-ing" endings.

He often used synesthesia to help us sing a certain way. "Imagine a glass of pineapple juice," he told the sopranos one day, holding an imaginary glass in the air. "Watch the pulp settle." Here, a finger-fluttering pantomime. "See how clear the liquid has become. Like delicate gold, transparent. Soprano Sisters, right here at the top of the glass"—finger jabs—"is where you sink." The sopranos sang there.

When the Texas City Explosion killed 581 people, several shocked families came to live a while at the monastery.

We served all comers in the Guest Dining Room at tables covered with white table cloths. Sometimes I was appointed to serve them. Since I spoke only English, I smiled a lot. And gestured.

Having guests at the monastery immensely pleased me. Benedictines have always emphasized hospitality. Fifteen hundred years earlier, Benedict had written in his Rule, "Let guests be received as Christ" and "Let the greatest care be given especially to the poor and to travelers."

Most guests stayed a few months and left, but the Skaupis stayed and Gorgy (*George* to us) gave us great music.

August always brought a scurry. Sisters left "home" to go to "missions" to teach or to do other work. The monastery felt empty. In September, Daddy came to see Lois and me. Mother had been dead a decade. Daddy, looking more and more Indian, had become an old man. Was this the man with bulging muscles who had pushed drill pipes to the bottom of the earth? The man who, when Mother Rita asked him if he wanted to work at the monastery, turned to me and said with tears in rheumy eyes, "We can be a family again!"

Bud left Subiaco and finished high school in Guthrie. He lived with Daddy in a room above the tool shed. We made a strange family. Two nuns who ate in the monastery dining room, a blond teenager who ate fast-food in his car, and our coughing round-shouldered Daddy who ate with the other monastery workers. It was the best we could do.

If the novitiate was supposed to prepare young nuns for mission life, it failed. At least for me.

When I'd sat on the boarding-school window sill in 1945 facing the prospect of finishing school and leaving the protective, if sometimes constricting, arms of boarding school life, what I had wanted was closeness to nature, song, and sense of doing good. I had believed that a little tucked-away monastic world was a source of grace in the world. I would serve others by praying and working and keeping the rules. That had been my conscious desire. I suppose that, unconsciously, what I'd wanted was a safe place to finish growing up. If I'd been a quicker learner, my experience as prefect of the boy boarders would have been a crash course in what the future held. But I clung to the ideal I'd formed while sitting on that window sill in 1945—an ideal reinforced in the novitiate.

All this is to say that when I went—with enough college credits to be teacher-certified—to teach at Marquette school in Tulsa, I was completely unprepared for the difference between mission and Motherhouse.

Sidewalks and playgrounds instead of gardens and orchards.

Rush instead of rhythm.

Prayer became something we had to "get in".

Unkind nuns.

That last difference—unkind nuns—was the hardest. There had been odd nuns at Guthrie—including Sister Alberta who, during lunacy episodes, was wont to climb into the sticky arms of cedar trees—but no one downright mean. At Marquette, however, four nuns (the "gang of four") seemed psychologically cruel.

As in all groups, the nuns at Marquette had unspoken rules:

1. Don't fail at your job.
2. Don't be too successful.
3. Whatever you do, don't outperform one of the gang of four.
4. Don't be too well-liked by parents or students.

In short, don't threaten the status quo. In the unfortunate case of excellence, punishment was meted out by means of exclusion, sarcasm, backbiting, and gossip. Meal times seemed to be the time favored for attacks. The gang of four often talked in the presence of the nun deserving punishment as if she were, say, a bowl of mashed potatoes. (I thought of Rita in Chickasha.) Leaving table was not permissible. A nun couldn't, therefore, throw down her napkin and stomp out the front door.

Unfortunately, Sister Wilhemena was both young and too creative. She was in charge of getting out a yearbook but, since she had no yearbook class, she and the staff worked after school and in the evenings.

The punishing conversation—the whoever-it-was diatribe—would go something like this:

"Did someone unlock the school last night around 9 o'clock."

"Yeah, and whoever it was sure was loud. It's a wonder somebody didn't call the police."

"I found potato chips all over the floor this morning. Whoever it was must've had a party of some sort. Surely no one thinks you can get work done while having a party."

"The lights were on till almost midnight. Whoever it was must think the electric bill is paid by magic."

"I heard Bill Martin's car peeling out about midnight. Isn't Bill the yearbook editor?"

"It must've been kids. No nun would let that kind of behavior go on."

I wondered if that's the way I'd end up someday. Would I grow to be 40 and mean and sit at table heavy in my darkness?

For some reason, I was never a target. Just as for some reason, I was never whipped at Chickasha. I have a slow-motion memory of being eight or nine years old and standing small in front of a looming Sister Evelyn in the linen room at the end of the dormitory. Sister Evelyn's face is red. She is saying, "Girl, I'll slap your face." I'm aware of a shapeless dark cloud filling the linen room. Sister Evelyn draws back her hand. Someone is beating a drum. The sound is deafening. I am saying—Where did the words come from?—"Don't lay a hand on me." She doesn't. She never does. In this memory, I walk out of the linen room. It's quiet. I realize the drum was my heart pounding.

Maybe whatever mysterious dynamic became operative in that boarding-school event also functioned at Marquette. Or maybe my escape was due to moral cowardice. Why didn't I say, "Quit! In the name of God, back off." But I didn't.

I was assigned to the Marquette mission seven years. My stomach hurt most of that time.

It never occurred to me to leave. My solace lay in the classroom. I had 40 students. I was 23 years old. My classroom was next door to one of the fork-tongued nuns. Talk about a drumming heart. Add watery knees! Thankfully, I had tucked away a little gem of advice about discipline, courtesy of one of the old nuns. "Just *expect* them to do what you say, and they will. If you doubt, they'll know." So when I said to my students, "Quietly take out your spelling workbooks," I fully expected 40 fourth-graders to produce spelling workbooks. And to do it quietly. They did. "If you doubt, they'll know."

Wearing a habit helped, too. It was, after all, 1950.

When June arrived after my first year at Marquette, I scurried home to the Motherhouse with relief. Even the occasional centipede looked friendly. Getting my hands in garden soil was therapeutic. Tomatoes needed to be picked. Corn needed to be shucked. Weeds needed to be pulled.

Farm life was healing. So was talking.

Martha was silent so long after I described the Marquette situation that I thought she hadn't heard. Had I talked too long? Finally she said, Zen-like, "If 20 men cross a bridge, there are 20 bridges." So? I thought. "So," she said as if she'd heard my mental prompt, "you don't have to end up like that." Of course I didn't have to become so bitter. Out of 18 nuns, four had shriveled like bitter raisins; the other 14 had crossed a different bridge.

Martha and I sat on the side steps hugging our knees. It was a clear June night. Stars were sharp as knives. Tulsa was 90 miles north. Marquette was a temporary assignment. But comforting talk at Guthrie helped only a little when I returned the next year. And the next. And four more after that.

During those seven years, Lois would finish nurses' training and be assigned to the little hospital in Guthrie. Bud would join the army. Daddy would die. And I would find our other granddad.

Dying of lung cancer is awful. Bud knew because he'd worked beside Daddy and slept in the flop houses. We watched Daddy struggle, writhe in his struggle for breath. Sometimes he'd grab my arm and twist as if my wrist held the last air in the world. The three of us were helpless to help the man we called Daddy. When we talked, we almost whispered. Bud, on leave from the army, described how Daddy, with a third-grade education, had worked menial jobs and lived in flop houses so he could pay for our tuition and milk and music lessons. "He loved us a lot," Bud murmured. All that time, I had thought he'd abandoned us. Left us to Aunt Rachel. Left us to fend for ourselves. I wanted to tell him I was sorry for my resentful feelings. I wanted to say Thanks. But he had gone past hearing.

In his wallet, we found a five-dollar bill and his wedding ring.

Daddy was buried in the Monastery cemetery. Bud hadn't been in the army long enough to have put money aside and Lois and I had no money, so none of us could afford a grave marker. If it hadn't been for Sister Ursula, Daddy's grave might have remained bare. Sister Ursula had kept up a correspondence with a former Monte Cassino student, Phyllis Isley. Phyllis had moved to Hollywood and become known as Jennifer Jones, the actress who played Bernadette in *The Song of Bernadette*. I'm not sure what Sister Ursula wrote to her former student, but Jennifer Jones bought Daddy's tombstone.

Back at Marquette after Daddy's death, I had the sense of teetering in the top branch of our family tree. Then I remembered the granddad who had sent us the doorstop, the one who had brought pink cheeks to Mother, the one with the funny name who lived in a town with a funny name.

The letter I wrote was addressed to "Mr. Jack Kitchen; Paw Paw, Michigan," and it began, "Dear Mr. Kitchen, If you get this letter, you might be our grandfather." He got it.

When Grandfather Kitchen came to see us, he walked tall and erect and used a cane with a silver collar engraved with *J K*. He had thick silver hair. He was amazed to find us Catholic. We were just as amazed to learn Mother had been reared Catholic. Could we have inherited a Catholic gene? He told us things we didn't know: that Paw Paw was a "little burg" in which the post master knew everyone by name—"which is why I got your letter"; that he'd remarried and had a son, Jack; that he still lived in the house Mother had grown up in; that we should come to Michigan for a visit.

The June following Grandfather Kitchen's visit, Lois and I got permission to travel with Bud—who had two weeks' leave and a rattling Ford sedan. The three of us were off to see our new granddad and, more importantly, to peek into our mother's girlhood.

When we drove into truck-farm country, we marveled at the ruler-straight rows: lettuce, onions, beets, carrots. Our grandfather raised asparagus.

The house was two-story frame, sternly rectangular. Mother's room was up a narrow flight of stairs. It had been used as a guest room, as it was now for her daughters. An antique pitcher claimed the wash stand. A hand-stitched quilt, the bed. Our mother may have looked out over the same green-striped fields though these same damask-curtained windows. One Paw Paw tree had grown tall enough to peek through the window. As if looking for someone.

After supper, Grandfather Kitchen's son, Jack, came over. Except for bad teeth, he bore an unsettling resemblance to Mother. We sat, a bit too stiffly for "family," while Grandfather Kitchen told his daughter's children about their mother and her mother, his first wife, a beautiful French Canadian who had died young. Except for Grandfather's voice and the mantel clock's ticking, the room was quiet. Too quiet. Grandfather's new wife, a lovely dumpling of a woman, seemed uneasy. Their son seemed downright unfriendly. He clearly wasn't interested in history that wasn't his history.

The clock ticked in his world, not in ours.

Back in Mother's old room the following morning, I walked over to the window. Trees. Fields. Gardens a quarter acre square. Mother had left this lush world for hardpan and slush pit. She must have loved Daddy very much. I tried to feel her presence, but too much was gone.

We heard from Grandfather Kitchen the following Christmas. After that, nothing.

After Marquette, I was assigned to teach high-school English, theology, and civics at St. John's School in McAlester, Oklahoma. Life at the convent was relaxed. Even jovial. The nuns were kind. Sister Mary Bartholomew, principal, taught the math courses. Sister Albert taught science. The teaching load was heavy, but I loved it. I didn't mind giving myself a crash course in civics so I could better teach it—not just stay a page ahead of the students. But I panicked when Sister Mary Bartholomew assigned me the job of helping the students learn "Battle Hymn of the Republic," "*Panis Angelicus*," and other pieces "in four parts so they could join other Catholic high-schoolers in Oklahoma City."

—No, I can't do it. I can't read music.

—You took piano lessons, didn't you? Anyway, you *have* to do it.

I continued to protest. It'd be dishonest. Pretense all the way.

—You'll be okay. Sandra will accompany. Do you want these kids to have to stay home from the big doin's?

She was the principal. And, of course, I didn't want the kids at St. John's School to miss the rally in Oklahoma City. So with my unseen knees trembling, I lifted my right hand in the air and explained to the reluctant songsters that they'd need to watch my hands closely in order to commence on the *and* of *one and*. We began by learning each separate part of *Panis Angelicus* by rote. Altos. Sopranos. Bass. Tenor. Then Sandra (who would later perform as a concert pianist) asked the fateful question, "Sister, shall I play the entire score so they'll recognize it?"

"By all means," I lied. "Listen carefully to the introduction, students. Watch my hand." I think I remember this event so vividly because it was an anomaly. As a rule, we were well prepared for teaching.

So Sandra leaned over the piano like a contestant at a watermelon-eating contest and played five measures of thunderous opening chords. I lost the place somewhere after the second measure. My hand froze in mid-air. Sandra stopped and looked at me quizzically. "We cannot begin," I said sternly, "until all—I repeat, all—eyes are on me." I glared at an imaginary eye-wanderer in the back row. Somehow we bumbled through. The kids even sounded good.

At that time, Catholics made up 3% of the population in Oklahoma. The lack of numbers made gatherings like the one in Oklahoma City doubly important to outlying communities. When a handful of Catholic students saw what must have looked to them like half the state's population, they surely felt less isolated, maybe more empowered. The songfest was magnificent.

Actually, St. John's students were natively musical. The school, located in McAlester, served kids from both McAlester and Krebs. Many were descendants of Italians who, in the 1880s had left Europe and come to mine the rich deposits of coal in the Krebs-McAlester area of Indian Territory. They were beautiful, musical kids with beautiful, musical names.

> Even after I knew their names
> I continued roll call.
> It was like reciting poetry—
>
> Regina, Belinda, Annunziata,
> Nemo, Como, Fabio.
> The ground below the school held
>
> tunnels hollowed in the 20s by miners
> named Dante, Valentino, Romeo.
> Poets. Singers. Lovers.

Late in second semester. Beppe
(aka Guiseppe) showed me
a grassless acre beside the ball diamond.

Nothin' grows here This ground's like a oven.
Know why? An old coal mine's burnin'
down there. Beppe's granddad had

died in the Krebs # 11 mine accident
along with a great-uncle
and the two Spanish mules

who'd spent their blind lives
pulling pit cars to the tipple.
At quitting time, the miners,

dead-tired with coal-dust faces,
emerged from the shaft
blinking in the late daylight.

But after supper they dug down
and brought to the surface concertinas
on which they played old Italian tunes.

In those days, Krebs flourished—thanks to coal. The Mississippi, Kansas, and Texas Railroad formed the Osage Mining Company and regularly whistled to a stop to feed on the black stuff. Both " The Katy" and "The Nellie," as locals called the passenger trains, carried local citizens to area towns. Being mostly Catholic, the Italians immediately set about building a church, St. Joseph's. Since music ranked just below religion, they then set about building an Opera House. When the frame church burned, the never-say-die Italians erected a brick church. It was completed in 1903. Today St. Joseph's stands almost unchanged. The Opera House also burned and was also rebuilt . Of brick. An Italian Band formed. On weekends, the band played on one of the double-decker bandstands built throughout the area. The interurban system made it easy for people from Hartshorne, McAlester and North McAlester, Wilburton, Carbon, and other towns in that area to gather to dance the night away.

When Osage Mine # 11 exploded in 1892, more than 100 miners died. Almost every family was touched by grief. Husbands. Sons. Fathers. Some bodies could not be identified. The Church could not accommodate that many funerals in so short a space of time. Besides individual graves, a mass grave was dug in McAlester.

When I was teaching there, all that remained of that heyday were memories and family records with gaps.

Maybe the home-brewed beer called Choc had been carried over from those early days. Awful stuff. Pffat! Since the Krebs-McAlester area lay inside the Choctaw Nation boundaries, and since Krebs took it name from Judge Krebs of The Choctaw Nation, I presume the nasty-tasting stuff came from the Choctaws. Whatever its history, Italians loved to make it. A sophomore girl told me that once her great-grandmother had been outside cooking Choc in a big black kettle on a wood fire when she spotted a revenuer. The quick-thinking law-breaker grabbed a laundry stick and tossed a pair of her husband's overalls into the foaming kettle. The girl finished the story with dramatic gesticulation, "She stirred like crazy. The guy must've thought those overalls were mighty dirty. Hops stinks, you know!"

I loved my three years at St. John's in McAlester. One thing happened, though, that nudged me nearer the exit to lay life. When Red Cross workers sent out a plea for volunteers after a tornado created havoc in Wilburton, Sister Alma told me I couldn't go help. "You'd miss Vespers," she explained.

At one time, I would have thought praying Vespers was important enough to take preference over action. I would have imagined our chant falling like rain, bathing the world. But when Sister Elizabeth told me I couldn't drive a few miles to help people in distress, I felt incredulous. In fact I felt ashamed. When had my thinking changed?

In the summer of 1955, Mother Paulinus called all the Sisters together in Chapter to decide whether we should stay in Guthrie or pull up stakes and move to Tulsa. Many or most of us were taken completely by surprise.

Leave Guthrie?

The nuns who favored relocating pointed out that, in 1879, Mother Paula O'Reilly's vision of a Benedictine Motherhouse had been drawn from Europe at a time when Christians—which in medieval Europe meant Catholics—gathered and built villages around hill-top monasteries. The village-towns and the monasteries grew together It was a reciprocal relationship in which both villages and monasteries flourished. The argument went this way: "But that was back there, back then. How many Oklahoma Catholics have flocked to Guthrie?" The obvious answer was none.

Not only was the community having no obvious influence in Oklahoma, but it was in debt.

The Chapter meeting lasted a long time and was very emotional. Centuries ago, St. Benedict had stipulated that anyone who had anything to say, pro or con, could speak "because the Lord often revealeth to the younger members what is best." Lois was a younger member. She spoke against the move.

We voted by dropping beans in a jar: white beans to stay, red beans to move. I reluctantly dropped a red bean. Reluctantly because the monastery at Guthrie had become my home. The community was my family. With its fields, gardens, orchards, the barn, the monastery in Guthrie had become my beautiful country home. I'd lived there ten years. But the farm in Guthrie was, quite simply, financially unsustainable.

One argument in favor of moving was that many of Tulsa's oil-rich families were Catholic and generous. They would help us financially. The decision came down to a choice between head and heart. Head won.

The move was wrenching. Nuns walked the lanes, picked the last pecans in the orchard, fingered the grave markers in the cemetery, even gazed on Lake Placid and found it lovely. I cried and cried. In Tulsa, Monte Cassino boarders were notified that the following year the boarding school would be closed. In Guthrie, Sister Joachim marked and arranged Guthrie's monastery goods for an estate sale. Many items had been purchased by Mother Paula O'Reilly back in 1889. Some, of course, were worse for wear but many were genuine antiques, and rich women from around the state came to buy.

Finally we loaded our narrow iron bedsteads—also antiques—and rattled up Tulsa's ritzy South Lewis Avenue looking, no doubt, like the Joads in habits. It was June, 1955. I was 27 years old.

We moved into a mansion on a large estate on 31st an S. Lewis. A winding staircase ended in a marble foyer. We crammed our little dinky beds wherever we could find an empty spot. Without a full-time yard man, the grounds became ill-kept. The neighbors must have been dismayed. From the mansion, we walked to the Monte Cassino chapel for community prayer. Hot weather felt hotter in that city of cement. Our sweat-dampened coifs drooped. Often I felt like I was wearing a goose-necked lamp. The chapel was air conditioned and so roomy our voices bounced off the walls, thin as wasps. I never thought I'd miss the too-small chapel at Guthrie, but I did.

In my mind, the move was a spiritual disaster.

Guthrie's Benedictine community—even the four unkind nuns—had become my family, the farm my family's homestead, the elegant poverty my family's social condition, hospitality and learning my family's values. Regardless of where I had taught, Guthrie had been both my point of departure and my point of return. We might leave to work in the 20th century, but we came home to a 16th-century monastery in Guthrie.

The family I'd thought I had began unraveling. Sister Mary Placida died soon after the move.

After the move, the years began to tumble. The stretch of years between seeing white chickens in the front yard at Guthrie and casting my vote to move had seemed unhurried and airy. In fact, in my memory, the Novitiate Year expanded much as Proust's first bite of the tea-dipped madeleine filled pages. That single novitiate year seemed a decade long.

Even today, when I think of Guthrie, I feel as if I'm inside a bubble in time where there's a garden, the rhythm of seasons, a haywire water pump, silence, a leaning barn.

I was assigned to teach at Bishop McGuinness High School in Oklahoma City. When the Motherhouse was in Guthrie, I had seen the rhythm of going out on mission and coming back to reinvigorate the spirit as a kind dance. Forward-back. Forward- back. That dance stopped after we moved to Tulsa. There was no coming back to a farm. The months formed a spinning pinwheel. Time kicked into high gear. The community seemed to flail. At least, I flailed.

Was the fast pace due to urban life versus rural? Twentieth century versus 16th? My age?

Confusion and unrest rippled through the scattered community—a kind of echo of rumblings in America. Martin Luther King had stepped on the world stage. Suddenly nuns were discussing social justice issues, particularly the race relations. It was an issue not unknown in Tulsa.

Tulsa's history began with the discovery of oil. Almost overnight, that discovery turned the former cow town of Tulsey into Tulsa, "Oil Capital of the World," a beautiful city that would quickly become known for both its sophistication and its philanthropy. During Tulsa's heyday period, oil barons built mansions, and probably the nation's wealthiest group of Black Americans built Tulsa's Greenwood district. It was as if two abutting towns lived together without incident. Until 1921.

If the Drexel Building's elevator operator, Sarah Page, had not stopped the elevator a fraction of an inch short of the floor causing black Dick Rowland to trip and fall against her, and if he hadn't fled when she screamed, the fragile demarcation might have held. As it was, the Tulsa Race Riot of 1921 erupted into America's costliest riot. (And also the most violent if, as some claim, the number of dead was not the official report of three dozen but rather 300, many buried in mass graves or thrown into the Arkansas River.) Who knows what part the Klu Klux Klan played in the riot. What's clear is that about 2000 Kluxers lived in the Oil Capital of the World in 1921. The National Guard finally turned a machine gun on the rioters. When the riot ended, 35 blocks in the Greenwood district lay burned.

Dick Rowland, whose accidental stumble against a white woman had set off the riot, was never charged.

When Mother Paulinus said I should go to Washington D. C. to begin work on graduate degree in literature at The Catholic University of America, I was elated. I was eager to learn more and to have time to read. Maybe the time away, I thought, would provide the distance to come to terms with the change from rural monasticism to convent life in an urban setting.

"It's an overnight trip by train," Mother Palinus said.. "Here's a quarter. You can rent a pillow." I turned the quarter over in my palm. And over again. It felt smaller than I remembered. But heavy enough. Solid. I hated to part with it.

When dusk fell, the train window became part mirror. I lay back and watched the landscape flow through my faintly mirrored head.

Like dreams slipping away.

Besides the quarter for a pillow, I had $10 for spending money. That summer—and, indeed, the next four summer sessions—I spent most of my spending money on bus tokens. Almost every day I traveled by bus to the Library of Congress. Partly to study but honestly mostly because, in those pre-air-conditioning years, the high-ceilinged Library of Congress offered a spot of relative cool. The habit was hot. In Guthrie, we wore cotton habits in the summers. "Cotton?" exclaimed a nun in one of my classes who hailed from Minnesota. "We wouldn't dream of wearing cotton. Serge, maybe, or gabardine. But cotton, never." I looked at her French wool habit and thought, You've probably never wrung the neck of a chicken, either. The more I talked with nuns from other parts of North America, the more the uniqueness of the monastery in Guthrie became clear. I felt sad that Oklahoma seemed so unaware of us.

When I returned from the first summer session at Catholic University, Lois asked for a dispensation from her vows. The dispensation came from Rome. I was devastated but not surprised. She'd been unhappy a long time, and I wanted to support her in her decision. But after Mother's death she'd become the family remnant who helped me know who I was. Who would I be without her?

I got permission to visit her in San Antonio. My sister in her own apartment? Wearing street clothes? Buzzing down the streets in her own car—a red Mustang, no less? In the convent, she'd taught nurse students at St. Anthony's Hospital in Oklahoma City. In San Antonio, she taught nurse students at Trinity College. Doing what she'd done in the convent and being paid? She seemed confident. She seemed fine without her big sister. When I waved goodbye at the airport, I felt as if I had left something behind. The feeling persisted even on the plane. I remember rummaging through my bag. Had I forgotten something?

During the third summer of study in Washington, an intense sexual awakening surprised me. My body seemed electrified. I fed the sensations with sexual fantasies. Or maybe it was the other way around: the feelings fed the fantasies. It was maddening. What was I to do with all this sexual energy? I was almost 30 years old. I was a nun. In a habit. I'd made a vow. In the cafeteria, I looked around at all the other nuns and wondered if any of them were feeling the same sensations. When I wasn't frightened by the sensations, I was pleased—even proud—to know my body was so terribly, beautifully alive. I was a woman. But was I worthy to be a nun? I remembered an orderly at the hospital in Guthrie who'd thought *nun* was spelled n-o-n-e. He thought it referred to gender. Could God really be pleased with a none-sex?

My confusion deepened the day a little boy on the bus stared at me bug-eyed, then pulled frantically on his mother's skirt and asked loudly, "Mom, Mom, is she a real witch?"

Fever-faced in my room that night, I mentally replayed the incident. It conjured another memory: a man on a street in Tulsa had glared at me with naked hatred, drawn close, and spat. I had fumbled for a hankie and wiped my flaming face. Everyone on the sidewalk suddenly became an audience. I began to feel uncomfortable wearing the habit I'd been so eager to get.

"The trouble with habits," a friend of mine was fond of saying, "is that women are round and habits are square." We laughed, but such comments jibed with research I'd been doing on the psychology of dress, namely that voluminous clothing keeps others at a distance and makes it easy for the wearer to stay wrapped up in self. I learned that most religious habits originated in the Middle Ages when dedicated women wore the dress of those they served. Peasant dress made them approachable to the peasant population. As far as I could determine, medieval women's dress styles changed over the centuries but somehow the nuns' garb remained unaltered and became the habit. Frozen in time. Why?

Enter Rome. For the first time, I began consciously to resent the fact that a group of never-married Italian men regulated the life style of nuns, including approval of what the women wear.

The research I'd been doing on clothing and other topics was for my first book, *Sisters for the World*. I had written some articles inspired by social science as it applied to women religious, and one of the editors of Herder and Herder had invited me to expand the ideas into a book. Actually, the book became search for a new identity for nuns; it described a way to let service in the 20th century flow from contemplation.

A few days after I related to Martha my shame at being seen by the little boy as a witch, she suggested a drastic plan. I was hesitant. What if we got caught? Martha assured me we wouldn't. Who'd be up at 4 o'clock.

At that time, I was teaching at Monte Cassino in Tulsa. At first, I hated teaching there because most of the girls came from wealthy families and I was prejudiced against the rich. But I learned that many of the kids' problems were not unlike the problems less affluent high schoolers had. Their mothers died. Their families lost their homes. They fell agonizingly in love. They felt the sting of sarcasm. The junior class had begun an outreach program that included collecting clothes. It was exactly what Martha and I needed to carry out the Plan.

Martha signed out one of the two cars—from 4 a.m. to 6 a.m. At 4 o'clock we dug through the box of donated clothes and found dresses, shoes, and one pair of clip-on earrings. We changed in the school bathroom, and drove to town feeling giddy and almost indecent. Almost sinful. Martha had found a dime. Dimes were easier to find on city sidewalks than in monastery orchards. We walked down the early-morning streets of Tulsa in borrowed clothes and ill-fitting shoes. The marvel was that no one stared at us! Not even a second glance. No one on the sidewalk suspected we were two nuns in mufti. After walking past an all-night diner a few times, we mustered enough courage to go in. Martha spent the dime on a cup of coffee. "I'm not thirsty," I lied to the waitress. We took turns sipping the coffee and wearing the earrings. We beheld ourselves in the shiny napkin holder. If the waitress glared at us, it was because we didn't leave a tip. That was it. Innocent, really. We drove home, changed back into our habits, returned the items to the Poor Box, went to chapel and then yawned through Mass.

We repeated that derring-do twice more just because it felt free.

In 1961,Mother Paulinus, crushed by our unpayable debt, resigned. I didn't know much about the financial condition of the monastery. One Sister told me that the bishop who'd promised to pay for the college building had died, and the new bishop was not inclined to give us such a large portion of diocesan funds.

Sister Johnita, a beautifully healthy and competent woman, was appointed to lead us through the 60s. In America, the 60s meant the Civil Rights movement, the Vietnam War, the Beatles, generational ruptures in families. For Catholics, add Vatican Council II to the tempestuous list. For the nuns from Guthrie, add unfinished adjustment from a country monastery to city housing. A tsunami of change seemed to threaten every structure. Mother Johnita's task was to be the Moses who would hold back the raging water. An impossible task.

One of the first things Mother Johnita did was build a dining room large enough for all of us to eat together. And, of course, we prayed together in the too-large chapel.

But, to me, it didn't seem like a monastic life. I missed the sky, garden, manual labor, meadow larks. Besides that, no amount of eating and praying together could stop the onslaught of the 60s.

Like the population of Americans in general, the population of nuns was split. Status quo versus gung ho. Fear versus excitement. Tradition versus reform.

When my book was published, some of the Sisters were scandalized. They branded me as a rebel. I heard that Sister Roseanne hurled the book against a wall and Sister Imogene reacted to it by bursting into a two-day crying jag. It didn't help that I was invited to speak at conferences across the country. I wasn't used to hostility. I had been one of the quiet, good Sisters, who had done her job unnoticed. Suddenly I had become a traitor. My reaction to negative opinions surprised me: I didn't care. In fact, a kind of stimulating contrariness filled me. I walked taller, more erect, stiffer spined. Perhaps the feeling was similar to the response my mother had had toward her father when he had disapproved of her engagement to my father. Just as her rebellion did not lessen her love for him, neither did my thinking lessen my fondness for the nuns with whom I'd shared so many years of my life. I think both my affection and my not caring served as a kind of armor. The Sisters who were upset grumbled about me and my book, but no one complained to me.

With Mother Johnita's permission, some of our Sisters participated in local peace movements, marching, making posters, passing out leaflets, singing "We Shall Overcome," "I Shall Not Be Moved" and other rally songs. Some Sisters marched from Selma to Montgomery.

"Getting plastered all over the newspapers," sputtered Sister Stanislaus.

Mother Johnita permitted five of us to live according to the plan for renewal outlined in my book—a plan that called for praying together, living in an integrated neighborhood, getting down and dirty in real service to the poor, and wearing clothes that didn't set us apart and above.

Those changes—involvement in social justice issues, living among and ministering to the very poor, optional habits—terrified the already frightened Sisters. The fear was basic. Their very survival not only as Catholics but also as nuns seemed threatened.

Their Church had become foreign to them. The Mass was in English with "the priest looking right at you." Communion was taken in the hand. Where were the mystical rituals? Latin? Communion rails?

The semi-cloistered, conventual way of life they'd known—some for 40 or 50 years—was gone. Young nuns were running around "showing off their legs" and hair. It was too much. Too fast. They complained and their complaints were heard in one of the many offices in the Vatican.

As a result of frightened complaints, one day Mother Johnita opened a letter from Rome which said, in effect, "You're fired!" It went on to say a Sister Fabian from a community in Chicago would arrive shortly to take over leadership. Stunned, Mother Johnita removed her habit and went home to Kansas.

A number of us were incensed at the injustice toward Mother Johnita and the interference from Rome. Outrage burned hotter because of the sense of helplessness. It was no easier for a handful of nuns to fight the Vatican than for a single citizen to fight the proverbial City Hall.

In Oklahoma City, the priest at the bishop's office, although sympathetic, said we could do one of two things: 1) Take it, or 2.) Leave it.

When the nun from Chicago arrived and scheduled a chapter meeting, I—who'd been too timid to speak against injustice at Marquette—stood up in my knee-length skirt and said, "I will not stay in the community because I believe that to stay would be to condone injustice."

It was 1967. I was 39 years old.

Epilogue

Last April, when my husband, Gene, and I were visiting with two of his daughters about the Advance Directives our doctor had given us, the girls' questions about my blood relatives revealed how little they knew about me.

"You need to tell them about yourself," Gene said. I demurred. From my work as a therapist, I knew that verbalization often results in tears.

"You're a writer," Gene said. "Remember, your personal history provides a unique view of state history. Why not write it down?"

So I've written this much. In the process, I can more clearly see what people say about life: that it's a quest.

At 80, I Ask Myself, "What did you really want?"

To have a home.
To slice carrots into miniature suns in my own kitchen
To sit in a blue-cushioned chair reading poetry for an entire afternoon
        without feeling guilty.

To love a good man lively and limber when younger
        and still to love him stiff with age.
To wear my body easily,
        its small beautiful breasts, occasional freckle, its wrinkles.
To laugh often and loud, belly hurting, nose running.

To bear no grudge against my stroke-crippled body.
To wake each graced morning renewed.

To have a weathered backyard swing and birds at a full feeder.
To hear a wren draw its bow across the wind.

And I ask myself, Have you gotten what you wanted?

Yes. All.

Judith Tate O'Brien is the author of three collections of poetry: *Mythic Places; By the Grace of Ghosts,* co-authored with Jane Taylor; and *Everything That Is Is Connected.*

She has taught in Oklahoma more than 20 years. and is a retired Marriage and Family Therapist. She was a Benedictine Sister almost two decades in a monastery close to Guthrie, Oklahoma.

She and Gene, her husband of 30 years, live in Oklahoma City.

About the memoir, she says: "By definition it's based on memory and memory is always selective. My sister might remember our childhood a little differently and another Sister might remember the convent differently; each event evokes an individual emotional response. This memoir is a strictly honest account of my recollection of events and my emotional responses to them."